TREACY'S
ROUTES NORTH

TREACY'S
ROUTES NORTH

Patrick Whitehouse ARPS
and
John Powell CEng, FIMechE

GUILD PUBLISHING LONDON

ACKNOWLEDGEMENTS

Frontispiece:
Ais Gill viaduct on the last mile of the
climb to Ais Gill summit. Class A3 4-6-2
No 60082 Neil Gow heads the up
Thames–Clyde Express in 1960.

The authors would like to thank John Edgington of the National Railway Museum for his care, thoughtfulness and detective work in not only identifying many of the pictures but also picking out the many details of change and ensuring that these are properly described in the captions to them. Eric Treacy was closely connected with the work of the Museum in his capacity of a Council Member of the Friends of the National Railway Museum, an appointment made by the Secretary of State.

British Library Cataloguing in Publication Data

Treacy, Eric
  Treacy's routes north.
  1. Railways – Great Britain – History –
  20th century
  I. Title   II. Whitehouse, Patrick   III. Powell,
  John
  385′.092′4   HE3018

  ISBN 0-7153-8739-1

This edition published 1985 by
Book Club Associates
by arrangement with David & Charles Ltd

© Millbrook House & P. B. Whitehouse 1985

Typeset by Typesetters (Birmingham) Ltd,
Smethwick, Warley
and printed in Great Britain
by Butler & Tanner Ltd, Frome and London
for David & Charles (Publishers) Limited
Brunel House   Newton Abbot   Devon

CONTENTS

Introduction   7
The West Coast route   13
The East Coast route   67
The Midland route   109
North West to the Hebrides   147
On Shed   163

The up Royal Scot approaches Beattock
Summit about 1951 hauled by
de-streamlined Coronation Class 4-6-2
No 46241 City of Edinburgh of Camden.
No doubt the locomotive would work
through over the 401 miles from Glasgow
to Euston.
   The stock is mostly BR Mark I in
crimson lake and cream livery.

INTRODUCTION

On Saturday 30 September 1978, two special trains ran over the Settle & Carlisle route: they were called *The Lord Bishop* and *The Bishop Treacy*. It is rare for a railway enthusiast to be remembered with love by his peers but Eric Treacy was a rare man. Not only was he a caring Bishop of the Church of England but he was also one of Britain's finest railway photographers, a Man of God and a Man of the People. The two trains concerned were memorials in steam commemorating with joy the very things that Eric Treacy loved, the day culminating in a service on Appleby Station where he died on 13 May 1978 while photographing one of his favourite engines, the final steam locomotive to be built by British Railways, No 92220 *Evening Star*. If Eric Treacy had ever thought of a memorial, and this would have been one of the last things in his mind, something, somewhere on his favourite route to Scotland would have been near the top of his list.

The fact that Treacy rose to high office in the Church was not bureaucratic ladder climbing; his character and quality saw to that. He could and did say some most outrageous things from time to time, but like the religious theme he introduced to his speeches at railway dinners, or in his talks to societies, his outspokenness was always accepted because it was mixed with caring and sympathy. As enthusiasts and friends, we asked him to many functions and even if this was at great personal inconvenience he would come if his church duties allowed. Always his love of railways and of the men who worked on them came to the fore. An example of thoughtfulness towards others, was evident in his membership of the late Maurice Earley's Railway Photographic Society where everyone submitted one of his very best photographs which was placed in a folio and sent round by post for criticism and hoped for praise. Eric Treacy never missed a single entry, his pen mixed encouragement with caution, advice and wit: his prints were scarcely if ever bettered.

His concern in photography was for technical excellence and he added to this his tremendous love of the steam locomotive. He did not use today's 'improvements', long focus and zoom lenses, they were not in any case available for most of his railway photographic work or in the film size which he used. But he did take the basic concept of the locomotive or train and add the *picture*; his backgrounds were chosen with care and above all he

7

Early post-war days, either 1948 or 1949, with unrebuilt Royal Scot No 46141. The North Staffordshire Regiment (Camden 1B) attacks the climb to Camden with a down afternoon express. (No 46141 was rebuilt with a 2A taper boiler in 1950). The two arches on the left are original London & Birmingham Railway survivors of 1837 while the houses still show evidence of bomb damage.

did the whole exercise. He developed and printed his photographs with equal care to that given to his exposures, making sure that it was the best possible print which came to public view. On those of us who used 35mm cameras and took only colour, he would jokingly yet seriously pour scorn – we were 'only button pushers' he said. And he was right. Or mostly right. But his skill in making those pictures gave us all encouragement. Treacy knew *exactly* where to stand on the lineside; twenty yards away the picture would not have been there, his judgement was superb. To the old breed of photographers, taking shots of trains on four tracks at 70mph, his work may have been considered as innovation with moderation and somehow this summed up Treacy the man.

But all this has been said before and some hundreds if not thousands of his pictures have been published in magazines and books, most of the latter under his own authorship, so what is there left to see? The answer is a great deal. When Treacy died he left behind him some 14,000 negatives ranging from quarter plate down to 35mm mostly packed away in shoe boxes with no lists of subjects, no dates and no records. His photography was rightly for his own joy and who could have known in the late 1950s, let alone the 1930s just how the scene would change. Now, after six years, the negatives are in some form of order though dates have to be obtained by detective work and indeed some will never be known accurately. But what *has* emerged is that although by today's standards he used only few locations for most of his photography, the routes from England to Scotland, particularly in the 1950s, have been recorded in considerable detail. Not every station, every junction or every branch line, but certainly the general pictorial history of the routes with their atmosphere and background, much of which has disappeared completely under modernisation.

Excellent though they have been, most of Treacy's previous books have tended to lack any overall theme bar the love of the railway. Certainly we have seen trains thundering up through those magnificent settings of Lime Street cutting, Shap or Ais Gill;

The 11.15 Birmingham to Glasgow train passing Shap Wells intermediate block signal in 1948. The locomotive, Princess Class 4-6-2 No 46209 Princess Beatrice, is in very early BR blue livery with British Railways in full on the tender. The train is the booked formation of eight coaches including a restaurant car (an early 1930s vehicle) to Glasgow and four to Edinburgh.

Newcastle Central station, west end, from the north of King Edward Bridge. A York Class K1 2-6-0 No 62064 is moving from the goods lines onto the bridge with a mixed freight in the late 1950s.

Ex LMS Class 5 4-6-0 No 45499 leaving Fort William on a Glasgow train in the mid 1950s. The Mallaig train is creating a great puther in the station. No clean air Act then! This has all been swept away to accommodate the Fort William relief road and the station is banished to a much more inconvenient site about ¾ mile out of town. This scene too is a time of change with the LMS Class 5 4-6-0s about to take over from the ex LNER K2s, K4s and K1s on the Glasgow to Fort William section though the Class did not venture to Mallaig.

we have admired the light and shadow at Kings Cross, York, Carlisle and Princes Street, Edinburgh, and we have felt the grime or smelt the soot in the locomotive sheds, but the whole of these have not as yet been linked together showing just how superbly Treacy covered the changing years on the great routes north. Here his cameras have recorded not only motive power from original Scots to 25 kV electrics and Ivatt Atlantics to Deltics, but also, in their way just as important the changes in the railway scene itself. Most of this was not done deliberately but careful selection of the negatives running over the years has proved extremely fruitful.

The Waverley route is now only a memory while the Settle & Carlisle line – certainly Eric Treacy's favourite – hangs under a Damoclean threat of closure; motive power on all routes has changed out of all recognition. There is also virtual abolition of the loose coupled freight train as well as the closure of junctions and stations; all in all the recorder of 1939 could not seriously (and would probably not want to) believe his eyes today.

Apart from his photography, Eric Treacy's next love was the big steam locomotive and the men who crewed it. Time and time

Class A4 4-6-2 No 14 Silver Link at Grantham in 1948. Silver Link is still in LNER post war blue livery with chromium cut out letters and figures. The coach in the background has an E prefix to the number.

again, his reflections in his books have gone back to his trips on the footplate, his eye taking in not only the working of the almost human machine but also the scenery around him. The change of scene over the past 40 years is one of the most dramatic in the history of Britain's railways and the clock cannot be put back: Harold MacMillan's Wind of Change applied here as elsewhere. How better to record this than through the eyes of one of our greatest photographers? Allied with this, is a life-time's experience at the sharp end of the LMS, and later BR, motive power departments for John Powell began his apprenticeship at Derby working his way up to Traction and Train Crew Manager at British Railways Board. In passing, he had many years as a mechanical inspector riding locomotives of all conditions and sizes as well, positions in the motive power department at Manchester and in Scotland at Edinburgh, Aberdeen, and Glasgow. Thus we have been able to link two of Treacy's loves, photography and locomotives. Sadly, Eric Treacy died just as the Inter-City 125 HSTs were coming to the East Coast route but no doubt he would have found a way of placing them in his landscapes as he did with the Deltics; he said of them 'if we *must* have the dreadful things', meaning diesels, 'then at least these give an image of power'.

This book in recording an important era for the railway, also forms a fitting memorial to the man whose love of the railway and insight into the love/hate relationship between a locomotive and its crew, made him the Railwayman's Bishop.

12

THE WEST COAST ROUTE

Eric Treacy took up church work in Liverpool in 1932. It was a year of savage economic slump. It was also, for the LMS, a momentous year, for William Stanier came in from Swindon to be its Chief Mechanical Engineer in January, with a Board remit to produce a locomotive fleet which would be master of foreseen traffic requirements and at the same time bring high availability and real economies in the costs of fuel, depot servicing and works overhaul. The move was badly needed.

The West Coast route was a curious mixture of railway, reflecting in some ways its diverse origins as a through route. Northwards as far as Warrington it had the semblance of a grand design, even if it sprang from two separate railways linked by a third. But thence to Wigan it began life as two branch lines from the Liverpool & Manchester, while between Wigan and Lancaster it evolved from two successive add-on railways built by local interests to get rail access to the south. The Lancaster & Carlisle was promoted in large measure by the Grand Junction Railway with Anglo-Scottish traffic in mind, and was conceived in one piece. The terrain, however, always marked it out as a section on its own, which until the early years of this century warranted special locomotive designs to work it. North of the Border, the ex-Caledonian main line comprised a homogeneous trunk route only as far as Garriongill Junction (4½ miles south of Motherwell), beyond which point a number of purely local lines was strung together to get into Glasgow, first using Townhead, then South Side and Buchanan Street, and finally Central some 30 years later, as its terminus. While the Caledonian was something of a 'horses-for-courses' railway, it did not single out its Carlisle main line for special locomotive treatment; rather, it showed real difficulty in making up its mind what it wanted, and produced a considerable variety of locomotives in penny numbers for its trunk traffic.

The LNWR had, in its last eighteen years of existence, revolutionised its locomotive fleet under the direction of two men, George Whale and Charles Bowen Cooke. The first inherited Webb's Augean stables and made a powerful start with the cleansing process, while Bowen Cooke, armed with the Schmidt superheater, built on Whale's excellent foundations to produce a quartet of main line locomotive designs which for their size could stand performance comparison with anything in the land. The

13

Georges, Princes, Claughtons and 0-8-0s took over the main lines and set quite new standards. Of them, perhaps it was the 60-ton 4-4-0 Georges that were the brightest stars, handling expresses of over 400 tons south of Crewe with apparent ease and as a matter of course, with no thought of piloting. Even over the formidable climbs to Grayrigg and Shap Summit these brilliant machines were regularly taking trains of up to 360 tons before World War I. But this promise could not be sustained under the more difficult conditions of the inter-war years; by 1932 the older and smaller engines were going fast, and even the later superheated classes were coming under the torch. At the end of that year, only two of the gallant little 2-4-0 'Jumbos' were left, and in line with a decision to give no more general repairs to Claughtons, no less than 24 made their last journeys. The other one-time front line passenger engines, Precursors, Georges and Princes were on their way out. Their frames were fairly flimsy, and their endurance was not helped by the post-grouping removal of the centre crank axle bearings. By the 1930s they had been down-graded to secondary and semi-fast services and station pilots, and so Treacy recorded them – working to the North Wales coast (Llandudno Junction was ever a stronghold of the 4-4-0s, where they were stored in lengthy lines during the winter) or on fitted freights out of Edge Hill yard. Only the irregular exhaust beat of the superheater 0-8-0s

The famous Doric 'Arch', or more strictly a propylaeum, at Euston in the early 1950s. The arch was erected in 1837 and formed a fitting entrance to London's first main line railway station, the gateway to the north. The lettering was added about 1870. This view must have been taken from the Euston Hotel. The two taxis are very much 'London Standard' probably made by Austin at Longbridge.

The brand new rebuilt Euston station in the summer of 1967 with Class 86 electric locomotive No E3141 on 1H46, the 17.30 Euston to Manchester via Crewe. The train in the background, 1H44, is the 17.20 Euston to Manchester via Stoke. The full electric service had commenced on 6 March 1967 but the station rebuilding was not completed until the following year: it was officially opened by Her Majesty The Queen in October 1968.

The 'corporate image' has not yet taken over completely as the coaches, although in blue and grey livery, do not have the legend 'Inter-City' at the left hand end and the locomotives are still in electric blue with the BTC crest. In spite of the 'Modernisation' the track is still bullhead, laid new when the layout was redesigned for resignalling in 1965.

on main line freight continued to indicate a still-thriving design with little challenge; the need for modern freight power on the Midland Division was dire and absorbed a high proportion of the new locomotives.

North of Carlisle, the Caledonian could only be described as unimaginative insofar as the main passenger services were concerned. Timings were generous, but none of the multiplicity of 4-6-0 classes built for the route produced performances within sight of those of the LNW breed. Massive they may have been, but they were distinctly sluggish, and even on Beattock bank (on which they were invariably banked with anything over about 300 tons) they made no great fist of it.

Treacy's Liverpool scene in the early 1930s still showed strong LNWR influences, but change was evident, the inevitable outcome of nine years of predominantly Midland thought on both the operating and mechanical sides. It took the form of mainly proved Midland designs of moderate size, a flood of 4-4-0 Compounds and Class 2Ps, Class 4F 0-6-0s and 0-6-0 shunting tanks. It was considered that on the West Coast the whole passenger service could be tailored to the haulage capacity of a single Compound. The utter failure of this policy became

The departure side of the old Euston station circa 1951. Coronation Class 4-6-2 No 46250 City of Lichfield stands at platform 13 with an evening departure. The locomotive (from Camden Shed, 1B) is still in BR blue livery and the visible stock is LMS, though painted in the colour scheme of early nationalisation.

painfully apparent in 1927 with the design and production under near-emergency conditions of 50 Royal Scot locomotives by North British Locomotive Co in four months, using two building works and with delivery starting within five months of a firm tender and order.

A slightly hesitant start had been made, however, in producing more general purpose engines of up-to-date design which, in an environment of good coal, reliable maintenance and keen enginemen, were fully on top of current work requirements. In the fields of express freight and excursion work, the ungainly Hughes/Fowler 2-6-0s were doing sterling work, while the early 2-6-4 tanks were outstanding performers and capable of high speeds. The Fowler 0-8-0s (the 'Austin Sevens'), with even exhaust beat but much tinkling noise from the anti-vacuum valves when coasting, were well-liked by enginemen, though the design of their running gear was a disaster area. The new 0-6-0 shunters were good within their class, even if they could in no way displace the old LNW 0-8-2 tanks from the heavy hump shunting on the Edge Hill gridiron.

Such was the scene for which the new CME took responsibility.

A double-headed down express leaving Euston in 1948 with Class 5 4-6-0 No 44713 (from Crewe North Shed, 5A) then almost brand new, and unrebuilt Royal Scot No 6153 The Royal Dragoon. At this point the down fast line at the foot of Camden bank is outside the retaining wall supporting Hampstead Road bridge, with the slow lines and the up fast line on the other side of the wall under the bridge.

17

Royal Scot Class 4-6-0 No 6144 of Camden Shed on a down express near Kilburn High Road in 1937 or 1938. The locomotive was named The Honourable Artillery Company *but ran for many years with the nameplates covered.*

After the ordered pastures of Wiltshire it was a rough, thistle-strewn field. The next five years were to test his mettle to the full. The priority need was for something even more powerful than the Royal Scots on the London–Glasgow trains; elsewhere they could cope. Acceleration was in the air with the demise of the tacit 8¼ hour agreement between East and West Coast rivals for the London–Glasgow and Edinburgh trains, entered into following the 1895 Races to Aberdeen. Improved comfort standards were giving increased train weights and the 420 ton limit for a Royal Scot on the 1 in 75 of Shap and Beattock was no longer adequate. A locomotive was wanted which could take 500 tons tare unassisted, and in additon work right through between Euston and Glasgow without change.

The result was the Princess 4-6-2, first appearing in 1933. The Liverpool area did not see them until the 1935 batch, working in from Euston. Treacy seemed to find them aesthetically satisfying,

18

and recorded extensively their assaults on Shap and Beattock, on which they tended to be a little more sure-footed than their later sisters, the Duchesses. One gets the impression, however, that it was the Turbomotive – the unique steam turbine driven 4-6-2 – which took his fancy above all. Perhaps it was that its regular turn, the 17.25 flyer from Liverpool to Euston after working a morning down train, just coincided with Treacy's photography 'slot' in a busy day.

Most of the other Stanier designs were taper boilered improvements of Fowler classes, though sometimes the improvement was delayed in its arrival. The Jubilees made a very shaky start due to draughting deficiencies which compounded the high water consumption due to low superheat. Treacy probably risked having their shortcomings described in distinctly worldly terms as he pottered around the locomotive depot at Edge Hill. No such problems befell the ubiquitous Class 5MT 4-6-0s and 8F 2-8-0s, though the latter were not greatly in evidence on Merseyside at that time.

In 1937 came the magnum opus, the streamlined Coronation Pacifics (soon to be known as 'Duchesses' as further engines appeared). The new Coronation Scot train, with its 6½ hour timing between Euston and Glasgow, was a new feature of Treacy's visits to London and the Tebay–Penrith area. But there were other opportunities to photograph the big Pacifics in the Liverpool area, ranging from running-in turns from Crewe when

Crewe South Junction circa 1951. Princess Class 4-6-2 No 46209 Princess Beatrice on a down express which had left Euston at about 10.35. The destination of the leading coach is Workington via Barrow. The up Royal Scot is approaching on the up fast line hauled by one of the de-frocked streamlined 4-6-2s No 46221 Queen Elizabeth. All the coaches of the Royal Scot are BR Mark Is in pristine condition, including one of the full kitchen cars which were rather extravagant of space.

For some years, this scene has been completely altered, with all lines electrified, while in the summer of 1985 the rationalisation of the track layout does away with the 20mph speed limit: on new through lines this is now 80mph, with 50mph crossovers leading to platform lines.

new, to working the flyer during the Turbomotive's all-too-frequent spells in the works.

So it was to certain locations on the West Coast main line that Treacy naturally gravitated, places where the engines (any type from which a satisfying picture could be built round) were working hard, speeds were moderate, smoke effects were there for the asking, while at the same time the surroundings could illustrate the many-faceted panorama of the working railway. Tall LNW signals, permanent way staff pausing as the train went by, bridges, cuttings, station roofs, all figured in his pictures.

The exit from Euston was a natural; from the platform ends and through the points and crossings of the throat area, the train had to be lifted up a mile of 1 in 70/112/77 to Camden. Often the engine that had brought the empty stock in from Willesden – anything from a 'Cauliflower' to a 2-8-0 – would be noisily helping in the rear, to drop off at the top of the bank. But at the front end it was all smoke, steam and furious sound as a Royal Scot, Pacific or Jubilee applied its muscle to the train and burst

A beautiful pre-war shot circa 1937 of a then unnamed Patriot Class 4-6-0 No 5520 (later Llandudno) on an up express passing Wavertree, Liverpool. The third coach is Great Western and the train may be the Liverpool portion of a North to West express which joined with the Manchester coaches at Crewe. The locomotive in the background is an ex Lancashire & Yorkshire 0-6-0, LMS No 12230.

out from under Hampstead Road bridge on to the bank proper. It was not a moment for all-out effort, for a bad slip which pulled the fire about was no way to tackle the long, almost continuous drag up to the summit of the Chilterns before Tring. Bushbury men on the Wolverhampton trains approached it a little differently, however, and would put a Jubilee hard at it with ten coaches on its tail and no banker; they had a nine minute timing to pass Willesden and felt they had no alternative. Once over the top, Kilburn No 1 was about Treacy's limit; three miles out, the trains were doing close on 50mph and getting into speed before hitting the climb at Brent Junction, four miles further on. But the backcloth of London housing and sidings was hardly the stuff of his pictures. Of course not everyone could have access to the trackside as Treacy did, but by the late 1930s he was taking such splendid photographs, and had proved that he could be trusted not to put himself in danger on the track, that the powers that be were quite happy to grant his requests for lineside permits for locations that might be barred to others.

The easy grades and fast running over the next 150 plus miles to Crewe interested Treacy little. But he has left a number of interesting pictures of Crewe South Junction, of trains either leaving the station or passing through at 20mph and starting the ten-mile climb to Whitmore troughs. From his perch on a signal

21

A dirty and unnamed member of the LNWR Prince of Wales Class 4-6-0, LMS No 25756, leaves Edge Hill, Liverpool, circa 1937 on an eastbound stopping train. By this time, the Prince of Wales locomotives had been relegated to less important duties and many had been scrapped. Thanks to the war six managed to survive into BR days. Edge Hill station is very different today, all the roofs have gone while the original buildings were cleaned and restored to celebrate the Liverpool & Manchester Railway sesquicentenary.

LNWR Prince of Wales Class 4-6-0 No 25804 hauls a 'through freight' (one lamp at the chimney and one at the centre of the buffer beam) at Edge Hill on one of the complicated goods lines giving access to the 'Gridiron'. The three leading wagons are very badly sheeted!

gantry alongside the carriage shed and Crewe South shed yard, he has brought out the tortuous path followed by both up and down expresses, and which so nearly brought disaster headlines on 29 June 1937 when the Coronation Scot train on a pre-service press demonstration run, was whipped up to 114mph on the descent from Whitmore but was left with inadequate braking distance and hit the first 20mph crossover at 57mph. The 1985 remodelling of the layout has eliminated the need for such drastic reductions.

Treacy's next haunt was the Preston station area, lying close to the River Ribble. There was a 15mph speed restriction through the station, and sharp climbs out of the valley – short but at 1 in 101 up to Maudlands to the north, longer but rather easier southwards to Euxton Junction and Coppull. From Ribble Sidings, up trains could be photographed as they accelerated over the river with the elegant Park Hotel and its footbridge to the up platforms in the background. At the north end, expresses fought their way up and round the multi-track approaches past Preston shed, dived under a road bridge in the shadow of one of the loftiest church spires in England, and suddenly found themselves on very mundane-looking double track heading for Lancaster. Three minutes was the allowance to get by Oxheys box, 1.3 miles out, a counsel of perfection if ever there was one.

Liverpool Edge Hill station circa 1949 with rebuilt Patriot Class 4-6-0 No 45531 Sir Frederick Harrison of Edge Hill depot bursting out of the series of cuttings and tunnels from Lime Street. The locomotive was one selected to be painted in the experimental liveries of 1948, in this case light green. It appears to be still wearing this livery, albeit very dirty.

Probably the Bishop's favourite location in Liverpool, the top of the incline from Lime Street to Edge Hill in about 1947. Unrebuilt Royal Scot 4-6-0 No 6134 The Cheshire Regiment *hauls a local train probably heading for Manchester Exchange. The locomotive is in the 1946 LMS livery of black with straw and maroon lining and is shedded at Edge Hill (8A).*

Lancaster was Treacy's next vantage point, the south end of the station offering a sprinkling of heavy expresses pulling out of the up platform on to the main line over a nasty crossover on a well-canted curve to start the one mile pull at 1 in 98 up to Lancaster No 1; sometimes a banker was taken. It was an area which, fortuitously, seemed to bring Patriots into their own.

But it was the climbs to Shap and Beattock that gave Treacy his greatest opportunities. From Carnforth, almost at sea level by Morecambe Bay, the line climbed in 31 miles to a height of 916ft at Shap Summit in two stages, and then lost almost all this height in the following 31 miles to Carlisle. Both approaches could be gruelling, for locomotive and enginemen alike, and both needed to be right on top of the job. Before getting anywhere near Tebay, the train had to climb from Milnthorpe 13 miles up to Grayrigg, 4½ miles of it on grades as steep as 1 in 111/104/106, and if that had 'winded' the engine the driver had to decide how far he could recoup the boiler *and* make speed before rushing Shap proper, or whether he would do better to stop at Tebay for a helping shove. From Dillicar troughs up to Shap Summit were six miles of

The deep sandstone cutting and tunnels from Edge Hill to Lime Street station, Liverpool. LMS Class 5 4-6-0 No 44920, from Saltley shed, Birmingham, hauls an up express, carrying the reporting number W242, the 10.30 Saturdays only Lime Street to Bournemouth. The locomotive's tender carries the first BR emblem, the emaciated lion astride a wheel, and all the stock appears to be LMS, thus the year may be 1950.

unremitting slog, over four miles of it at 1 in 75, through bleak fell country where winds could be fierce, rain frequent, and ever-present risks of being checked or even stopped as preceding freight trains battled their way to the top with one of Tebay's Fowler 2-6-4Ts noisily bringing up the rear. Such was the potential bottleneck presented by the bank that the 5½ miles from Tebay to the Summit box was divided into no less than four block sections northbound, with intermediate block colour-light signals at Tebay North (often referred to as Greenholme) and Shap Wells, and between them the diminutive manned signalbox at Scout Green, controlling just its own four signals, the Shap Wells IB signals and a level crossing. Throughout the 24 hours it sat modestly amid the thunderous beat of hard-working engines and rattled to the vibration of south-bound trains coasting by at speed and bank engines returning to Tebay. There were curved

27

Ribble sidings, Preston, in 1948 with the penultimate Coronation 4-6-2 No 46256 Sir William A. Stanier, FRS heading an up express, probably the 09.05 Perth to Euston. The last two engines of the Class appeared under Ivatt's regime as CME and showed a number of detailed differences from the earlier engines.

An up express leaves Preston in early post-war days hauled by LMS Class 7P 4-6-2 No 6254 City of Stoke on Trent (Camden, 1B) in 1946 livery of black with straw and maroon lining. The train consists of at least 13 coaches but does not appear to carry any roof boards. The Park Hotel, now Lancashire County Council offices, is in the left background and Whitehouse West Junction on the L&Y line to Southport is behind the engine's left-hand buffer.

embankments striding over the fell, and a deep rock cutting approaching the Summit, spanned by a high steel bridge. What more could a dedicated railway photographer wish for?

Up trains also offered considerable possibilities. The start from Carlisle was heavy right from the station throat and could tax an engine coming on 'cold'. This was a favourite Treacy spot as expresses pulled up the 1 in 110 to climb over the goods avoiding lines, the North Eastern line falling and curving away on the up side for Newcastle and the Settle line. But further south were three more well-used locations. The first was the south end of Penrith station, offering not just main line trains restarting, but a wealth of locomotive variety; long-lived LNW Cauliflowers ran the Keswick trains until the late 1940s and there were small LNE pre-grouping types – J21s and GE E4 2-4-0s – heading over the Pennines to Darlington. Three miles south was the sweeping curve between Eden Valley Junction and Clifton & Lowther, with the long up goods loop alongside in which freights could queue for a path, nicely into the long 1 in 125 which stretched unbroken nearly to Shap station. And lastly there was the sinuous section past Bessie Ghyll intermediate block signals (sometimes known as Great Strickland, but never by railwaymen) and Thrimby Grange box with its up loop, the line wending its way through a wooded ravine in company with the infant River Leith. Speeds were seldom more than 40mph here, a smoky exhaust was almost guaranteed as the engine hammered uphill with wide open regulator and lengthy cut-off, and the superelevation offered pictorial possibilities.

North from Carlisle, drivers working to Glasgow were expected to know both the Caledonian route via Beattock and the South Western road via Dumfries, and to accept diversion at Gretna Junction without demur. Treacy was little diverted by the G&SW, however, and stuck loyally to the Caley main line. The ten mile bank from Beattock station to the Summit box, mostly at 1 in 75 or thereabouts, offered everything to the photographer – bank engines, magnificent pine-clad hills, open views across the valley floor, an intermediate signalbox with refuge siding (Greskine), the fine viaduct at Harthope, and above all, literally, towering exhausts. What a photographic paradise, as Duchesses and Princesses on Londons or the Birmingham–Glasgows, Scots and Jubilees on the Manchesters, a sprinkling of BR standard types, Class 5s on freight for Mossend Yard, and WD 2-8-0s and 2-10-0s on mineral workings, pounded up the hill, often with the tell-tale smoke and steam plume at the rear from the banker. In contrast to the train engine, it could have been a Caley 0-4-4T, a Pickersgill 4-6-2T, or a modern 2-6-4T – even once, in late 1960, a Kingmoor Princess! It could be an extremely difficult climb, seemingly endless, particularly with early morning mists, dew on the rails and much slipping. In extreme cases trains could stall; at

28

*Unrebuilt Royal Scot Class 4-6-0
No 6162 Queen's Westminster Rifleman
heads a six coach up local out of Preston
circa 1937. The signal gantries display a
magnificent array of LNW arms and the
coaches of the train are an equal mix of
LNW and LMS standard. A Stanier Class
5 4-6-0 is moving off in the left hand
background, beyond the permanent way
gang. The Royal Scot's smoke deflectors
are the penultimate design with an angled
upper portion. In the final design the top
of the plates were curved and followed the
contour of the smoke-box (see locomotive
No 6134 in the picture on pages 24 and
25). The whole train seems to be clean
and freshly painted red, with No 6162
carrying the Preston shed code, 10B.*

the other extreme it was not entirely unknown for the train to run away from the banker, and *that* could present a very tricky situation!

Further north, Treacy seemed never to have discovered anything that satisfied him sufficiently to spend much time there. The upper reaches of Clydesdale were delightful, with some attractive river crossings, but speeds were high and did not give rise to a lifting exhaust. The heavy industry and mining dereliction of the Motherwell area gave him no scope. Glasgow Central was no very impressive station architecturally. Only Princes Street, Edinburgh, with its high roof and attractive end screen seemed to strike a chord, and even that was less to his taste than the much larger Waverley ¾ mile away.

His pictures live as a tribute to the steam locomotive working in an attractive environment. It was perhaps not representative, for the photographer can pick and choose; he can revel in the

bright and shiny and decline, if he so wishes, to press the button when faced with a grimy engine leaking steam at many pores. Treacy was clearly frustrated by the end of steam. Class 40 diesels did little for him, and the era of twin Class 50s in 1970/1 failed to excite him unduly; even on the upper reaches of Shap the latter could be travelling at over 70mph yet looking quite lifeless, as if at rest. The paraphernalia of overhead electrification seemed to intrigue him briefly, as a novelty to be experimented with, but the portrayal of speed and power eluded him, as it has eluded practically every other photographer, and he confined his camera almost completely to static station scenes, introducing interest by human figures rather than the clean-cut outline of an electric locomotive. Pantographs and rooftop equipment were no substitute for chimneys and safety valves. Treacy was a portrayer of the living steam locomotive. Everything else could only be second-best.

The 09.05 Perth to Euston leaves Preston around 1950 hauled by Coronation Class 4-6-2 No 46237 City of Bristol (Camden 1B) in the early BR blue livery with red backing to the nameplate. The coaches are LMS but carry the first BR crimson lake and cream livery. The covered footbridge to the Park Hotel is visible over the end of the train. By this date, it was in effect a private exit for Lancashire County Council employees.

31

Preston again with unrebuilt Royal Scot No 46148 The Manchester Regiment leaving with a parcels train in 1950. The leading vehicle is an insulated van built specially for Palethorpe's of Tipton to convey sausages and pies to all parts of the country. The furthermost destination was probably Perth and this may be the Perth van returning to Dudley Port station. There is a nice mixture of upper quadrant and LNW arms adorning the gantry on the left.

Lancashire & Yorkshire Railway design Class 5P 4-6-0, LMS No 10448, allocated to Accrington, hauls a short train out of Preston and heads for the LNW main line in 1937. This may be a Barrow or Windermere portion off a Euston to Blackpool express. The locomotives, which were multiplied by the LMS, worked nearly all the important main line trains north of Preston until displaced by Royal Scots. They were a very short lived Class having an average life of 15 years.

No 10448 was always an LMS engine being built in July 1923 although its original number was L&Y 1677. It was one of the luckier members of the Class as it was not withdrawn until 1949.

The up Royal Scot passing Lancaster in 1951. The locomotive is a very grimy Coronation Class 4-6-2 No 46245 City of London (Camden 1B) and the coaches are of BR Mark I pattern. Lancaster Castle which gave its name to the station is just visible above the steam.

LMS Jubilee Class 4-6-0 No 45689 Ajax (Crewe North Depot, 5A) leaving Lancaster hauling an up express on the difficult climb of 1 in 98 to Lancaster No 1 signalbox. The train consists of two four-coach corridor sets in the first BR livery, with an extra van on the rear.

Patriot Class 4-6-0 No 45518 Bradshaw of Carlisle Upperby at the head of an up through freight passing Lancaster Castle and tackling the bank to Lancaster No 1. The date is around 1951.

LMS Class 4 2-6-0 No 43034 standing in the up yard at Lancaster in early BR days. The engine is pictured in as-built condition with double chimney and blast jets in narrow 'vee' formation. Steaming was very indifferent with this arrangement and after trials on the Swindon testing plant, it was replaced with a single chimney.

Oxenholme in 1951 with Patriot Class 4-6-0 No 45502 Royal Naval Division (Carlisle Upperby shed) departing on an up express, perhaps a Carlisle to Euston, which will join up with a Barrow or Blackpool portion further south. Note the wooden goods wagons in the yard and the light hand-operated crane, both sights of the past.

A down train hauled by Royal Scot Class 4-6-0 No 46116 Irish Guardsman *near Grayrigg*. (Grid reference SD579 962). This may be the 09.25 Crewe to Perth (the locomotive carries a 5A shed plate) and if so, the leading vehicle was a regular traffic in prize calves from Crewkerne LSWR to Maud GNoS which came via the S&D, Bath and Birmingham New Street. The stock is ex LMS and painted maroon so the date may be early 1950s.

A down partially fitted freight train approaches Grayrigg (to be precise 26 miles from Lancaster) hauled by LMS Class 8F No 48433 of Edge Hill shed. The engine had not been correctly prepared as there is still some smokebox char on the buffer beam which could blow back and finish up in the crew's eyes. Note the then new flat bottom rail and the cows ignoring the passing of noisy steam.

A named Class 40, probably No D221, hauling an up express over Dillicar troughs in the Lune Gorge in the early 1960s. The first Class 40s were built with air operated water scoops for picking up water at troughs to supply the steam heating boiler. They were later removed as with the withdrawal of steam the removal of water troughs, and the fitting of coaches with electric heating, the scoops served no useful purpose.

The Lune Gorge with an unidentified LMS Class 5 hauling down milk empties approaching Dillicar down intermediate block signal distant. Note the cyclist in the up cess!

Shap Wells about 1951 with a very dirty Coronation Class 4-6-2 No 46250 City of Lichfield on the Carlisle portion of the 10.35 from Euston with only six coaches including restaurant car and one van bringing in the rear. No bank engine was required for this load and the Duchess is taking it easy.

A view of a Duchess climbing to Shap Summit, taken from a highly hazardous viewpoint, probably on top of the coal in the tender or from a toolbox lid.

A pre-war shot which has been seen before but well stands repeating. Rebuilt LNWR Claughton Class 4-6-0 LMS No 6017 Breadalbane of Carlisle Upperby hauling a down freight at Scout Green near Shap Summit circa 1937. The exhaust steam from the bank engine can be seen above the platelayers' hut. All the unrebuilt Claughtons had been withdrawn by 1935 and the rebuilds had also started to disappear by 1937. In fact only one, No 6004, lasted through the war years and just into BR days.

The 11.15 Birmingham to Glasgow express approaches Shap Summit in 1967 hauled by two Class 50 diesel-electric locomotives Nos D411 and D442. The formation of the train, all BR Mark I stock mostly in blue and grey livery, appears to be seven Glasgow and five Edinburgh coaches.

Shap Wells about 1951 with LMS Class 5 4-6-0 No 44833 hauling a down express freight and banked by an LMS Fowler 2-6-4T. This photograph shows the wild country in the Westmorland hills, and the filthy state of engines running at the period generally; the cabside number is almost obliterated by dirt.

Another well-known photograph of the up Coronation Scot just south of Shap Summit, in the summer of 1937. (The locomotive and train look too clean for it to be 1938 or 1939). The train is formed of the booked nine coach set in blue and silver livery. The locomotive is the pioneer of the Coronation Class No 6220 Coronation. Milepost 37 from Lancaster and Shap Summit down distant can be seen on the left.

LMS Jubilee Class 4-6-0 No 45705 Seahorse on an up train of 16 ton mineral empties possibly near Bessie Ghyll on the northern climb to Shap from Carlisle. The locomotive carries the headlamps for a through freight. The shed plate 10B indicates a Preston engine.

The up Royal Scot near Thrimby Grange in 1955 or 1956 when Southern Region diesel electric No 10203 was on loan to the LMR. Not the brightest of weather and a day which Eric Treacy would have ignored but for the special nature of the event.

LMS Class 5 4-6-0 No 45185 of Carlisle Upperby hauls an up fully fitted freight at Clifton & Lowther. The photograph was taken in the late 1950s or early 1960s as the engine is fitted with AWS.

A Glasgow to Liverpool and Manchester express passing Clifton & Lowther double-headed with an LMS Class 2P 4-4-0 No 40694 of Preston and Britannia Class 4-6-2 No 70050 Firth of Clyde of Polmadie. The train is a fairly heavy one, probably 15 or 16 on, hence the pilot between Carlisle and Preston where the train would divide. The coaches are a mixture of LMS and BR Mark I stock and the picture probably dates from 1957.

Clifton & Lowther with a Class 40 No D332 hauling 1M22, the up Royal Scot 10.00 Glasgow to Euston composed of BR Mark I stock, around 1962. A Class 5 stands in the up loop with a train of 16 ton mineral wagons.

Clifton & Lowther in 1947 with LMS Class 5 4-6-0 No 5295 of Carlisle Upperby hauling an up partially fitted freight composed of a mixture of wagons, including meat containers next to the engine and forming the fitted head of the train. The signal is in the 'six foot' for ease of sighting round the curve and is an LNW post with LMS upper quadrant arms.

45

A photograph taken between Eden Valley Junction and Eamont Junction near Penrith showing the two LMS diesel-electric locomotives Nos 10001 and 10000 hauling the up Royal Scot in 1950. A J21 Class 0-6-0 on the down line heading a Darlington to Penrith train may well have checked the express at Eden Valley Junction's distant signal. The Royal Scot is still 100 percent LMS stock though apart from the leading van all coaches are in BR crimson and cream livery. The locomotives were the forerunners of all today's main line fleet, No 10000 itself being completed by the LMS in December 1947.

Penrith circa 1937 with an ex LNWR 18 inch goods LMS No 8345 leaving on a train for Keswick and Workington. The train includes a wonderful collection of pre-grouping coaches, plus an LMS fitted goods van next to the engine. It consists of an MR clerestory 48 foot lavatory brake composite, an LNW 45 foot arc roof lavatory composite with a small luggage compartment, and Furness 50 foot arc roof brake third, as well as a Midland six wheel clerestory brake van. In spite of its looks, the train did not have a high carrying capacity; there were only 21 first and 115 third Class seats.

Penrith in the late 1950s with a two-car Metropolitan-Cammell diesel multiple-unit on a Penrith to Darlington working. The dmu has just come through the two crossovers behind the train from the bay platform and is passing No 1 box.

Penrith immediately after the second world war with an LMS Class 5 4-6-0 No 5440 leaving at the head of an up through freight. No 5440 was a Bath (22C) engine and must have been running in from Crewe after a visit to the works. On the right of the picture is an LNW Watford 0-6-2T, almost certainly No 6883 which was the only one of the Class in the north after the war.

48

Keswick in the snow in February 1955 with a brand new Derby built diesel multiple-unit on Workington to Penrith duty. This batch of dmus had bars across the droplights and restricted sliding lights to prevent passengers putting their heads out of windows on the Maryport & Carlisle line which has restricted clearances.

A double-headed express passing Penrith No 1 signalbox. The pilot is LMS Class 2P 4-4-0 No 40565, attached at Carlisle as the train would be over a single engine load for the climb to Shap; the train engine is a rebuilt Royal Scot. The photograph can be dated between 20 April 1958 when Preston shed adopted the code 24K and November 1959 when 40565 was withdrawn.

An up express leaving Carlisle around 1958, double-headed with Patriot Class 4-6-0 No 45502 Royal Naval Division (Upperby 12B) and an unknown Jubilee 4-6-0. The lead into the former LNWR goods depot is on the right and passing under this is the NER line to Newcastle which was also used by Midland trains to Petteril Bridge Junction.

Carlisle during the reconstruction of the station roof about 1957. Royal Scot Class 4-6-0 No 46136 The Border Regiment (shed code 12B, Upperby) waits in the middle road for an up Lanky express. (The Lancaster & Carlisle line was and still is known in Carlisle as the Lanky). The Waverley has just arrived behind a Gresley Pacific and Jubilee No 45564 New South Wales is waiting to take over.

Carlisle station after completion of the alterations to the roof about 1958. A Derby-built two-car diesel multiple-unit waits at platform 4 to form the 17.05 to Penrith. Until the coming of the dmu sets, this was often an LNWR 18in Goods 0-6-0 working.

The north end of Carlisle Citadel station with a formidable line up of power in 1958. Jubilee Class 4-6-0 No 45643 Rodney (5A, Crewe North) is taking water at the down platform. Alongside are BR Clan Class 4-6-2 No 72008 Clan Macleod (12A Kingmoor) and another Jubilee No 45591 Udiapur on the right, both no doubt waiting to work north.

Facing page top:
BR Clan Class 4-6-2 No 72006 Clan MacKenzie leaving Carlisle and passing No 3 signalbox in the mid 1950s. Note that the draught sheeting between the engine and tender is torn and coming adrift. The Waverley Route leaves the ex Caledonian line on the right of the third to fifth coaches. The leading vehicle is a vintage LMS 12-wheel restaurant car of the late 1920s.

Right:
A pre-grouping period piece in early BR days around 1948. Caledonian Railway Mackintosh Class 3F 0-6-0 No 57621 heads a local trip freight (No K5) along the goods lines at Carlisle. The photograph was taken at Bog Junction with Rome Street signalbox in the background. The curve to the left was Maryport & Carlisle property and leads to Maryport. The train is on ex North Eastern Railway track.

Jubilee Class 4-6-0 No 45673 Keppel
(Perth shed) leaving Carlisle with a train
for Perth. Signals controlled by No 3 box
are clear for the main line. The filthy state
of the locomotive tends to a view that the
date is the early 1960s.

A down express hauled by a Class 40
diesel passes Etterby Junction in the early
1960s. There is evidence of the Carlisle
area multiple-aspect signalling scheme
near the signalbox in the form of a colour-
light signal which is fitted with a wire
mesh guard in anticipation of electrification although this was, in the event,
about 10 years away. The signalbox and
goods lines in the foreground were part of
a wartime scheme (opened in 1943) to
ease congestion at Carlisle.

Opposite:
Two Class 17 diesels, No D8529 and
another, built by Clayton of Derby, en
route for the Scottish Region on delivery
from the manufacturers in 1963, passing
under 'The Viaduct' at the north end of
Carlisle Citadel station.

Opposite:
Crossing the border. LMS Class 5 2-6-0 No 42736 on a down freight precisely on the boundary, the River Sark, south of Gretna Junction. Gretna station, ex Caledonian Railway, which closed on 10 September 1951 can be seen in the background. In spite of its name the station was just in England.

A down express, probably the 11.15 Birmingham to Glasgow passes Kingmoor shed, Carlisle around 1964. A line of stored engines to the left includes two Crab 2-6-0s, a Jubilee, a Duchess and a WD 2-10-0.

Kingmoor Carlisle a few years later, after the motive power depot had closed and the building used for storing carriages. On the down goods line heading for the new marshalling yard is Class 47 No D1880 at the head of a train of 100 ton oil tank wagons. The leading barrier wagon is a 32 ton merry-go-round hopper.

Opposite:
Beattock with Class 5 4-6-0 No 45482 about to leave on a fitted freight. The train consists of about 20 vans so would not require the services of a banker. On the right is the locomotive shed which supplied the bank engines for trains requiring assistance to Beattock Summit, mainly LMS Class 4 2-6-4Ts, and the Moffat branch engine, a CR 0-4-4T. The Moffat branch curves away to the left.

The bottom of Beattock bank with a freight train beginning to tackle the climb. The bank engine is LMS Fairburn 2-6-4T No 42213 still with first BR emblem; it does not appear to have a tail lamp.

Greskine signalbox on the 10 mile climb from Beattock station to the summit. A down local is passing hauled by BR Clan Class 4-6-2 No 72001 Clan Cameron of Polmadie shed, Glasgow. These engines, probably the least successful of the BR Standard Classes, were weak in relation to their nominal power: No 72001 is in nearly full forward gear on the 1 in 74. Possibly the train had been stopped by signals and was drawing up to the starter?

BR Standard Class 5 4-6-0 No 73061 of Motherwell on a down through freight (no doubt limited to lower category by the tank wagons) near Harthope on Beattock Bank. The train is banked by one of the last series of LMS 2-6-4Ts.

The 11.15 Birmingham to Glasgow climbing Beattock near Harthope in the mid 1960s hauled by Class 47 No D1842 which has scorned the aid of a banker. The train is now all BR Mark I stock except for the last two Edinburgh coaches which are LMS types. The formation is back to eight for Glasgow and four Edinburgh vehicles and the first class is designated by a yellow band over the windows. The hillside is now a Forestry Commission plantation.

Class 37 No 6853 hauling a train of limestone for Colvilles Steel Works, Motherwell, nears Beattock summit banked in rear by what must be a Class 20 diesel electric. The photograph dates from the early 1970s.

Harthope intermediate block signal approximately three quarters of the way to Beattock summit with LMS Princess Class 4-6-2 No 46209 Princess Beatrice heading the 11.15 Birmingham to Glasgow in the late 1950s.

The up Royal Scot approaches Beattock Summit about 1958 double-headed by the two Southern Region diesel-electric locomotives Nos 10201 and 10202. Note the Caledonian Railway catch point sign (white letters on blue enamel) beside leading locomotive.

Elvanfoot with Jubilee Class 4-6-0 No 45616 Malta G.C. on the 09.05 Perth to Euston about 1957. The locomotive rather surprisingly is from Kentish Town, the main Midland shed in London.
Elvanfoot was the junction for the highest branch line in Great Britain, to Leadhills and Wanlockhead, which left the main line in a trailing direction behind the goods shed.

The up Royal Scot near Crawford hauled by Class 8P 4-6-2 No 46221 Queen Elizabeth in 1957. The locomotive was one of the first two blue and silver streamliners built to haul the prestigious Coronation Scot 20 years earlier.

Carstairs Junction with an eight coach train of ex LMS corridor stock in early BR livery leaving for Edinburgh in the early 1950s. The locomotive is ex LMS Class 4 2-6-4T No 42145 of Carstairs. This is described by Eric Treacy on the rear of the print as a Birmingham to Edinburgh train, but it is twice as long as the booked portion to be detached at Carstairs and the roof boards on the leading coaches are reversed to show their blank side. When the Edinburgh portion ran as a separate train, it usually ran direct from Strawfrank Junction to Dolphinton Junction avoiding Carstairs. So we have an enigma.

Carstairs Junction in 1954 with an LMS Class 4 2-6-4T No 42173 and 0-4-4T No 55261 each shunting two empty coaches. The 0-4-4T was one of a batch of 10 built by Nasmyth Wilson of Patricroft for the LMS in 1925 to a Caledonian design. The locomotive shed can be seen on the right with concrete coaling plant beyond.

Edinburgh Princes Street, the Caledonian station, with BR Class 5 4-6-0 No 73059 of Polmadie leaving on an up express. It appears to be a short train so may well be the Edinburgh to Birmingham: the lack of a CR route indicator does not help in identification. Note that the locomotive has altered guard irons for the fitting of a miniature snow plough.

Edinburgh Princes Street with an ex Caledonian Railway Mackintosh 0-6-0, BR No 57550, leaving on a local train probably for Glasgow via Shotts. Today the magnificent roof has gone and the site of the platforms is a car park. Part of the station concourse has been taken into the hotel and is now a bar.

Glasgow Central with Jubilee Class 4-6-0 No 45642 Boscawen stationed at Newton Heath about to leave on a Glasgow to Manchester/Liverpool express. The Fowler 3,500 gallon tender is well stacked with coal for the 232 mile trip. Date about 1956. This scene is much altered now with overhead wiring and simplified track layout.

THE EAST COAST ROUTE

It seems to have been 1938 before Eric Treacy, having cut his teeth mainly but not exclusively on LMS trains on Merseyside, turned his attention, albeit on isolated occasions, to the East Coast main line in the Home Counties. He was still based at Edge Hill, and perhaps it was his budding acquaintance with the LMS Duchesses which roused his interest in the Gresley equivalent.

The East Coast route to Edinburgh developed as a three-railway partnership which lasted until the Grouping in 1923. It was a rather flatter route than the West Coast line, once it had breasted the eastern end of the Chiltern Hills beyond Welwyn – in fact, for the next 200 miles and more – it was a pretty dull countryside through which it ran, flat, with sluggish rivers and a dearth of sizeable towns. As befitted this countryside, it was laid out for fast running as far as Darlington, except through Peterborough, Selby and York. Once into County Durham, things deteriorated somewhat; tighter curves became necessary in the more broken country that stretched, with little relief, to the Scottish capital, and with them came a plethora of speed restrictions, mostly not very serious for steam locomotives but rather more so with diesel traction. The main climbs, often at 1 in 200 or so, could generally be rushed at good speeds, and were seldom of any great length. Instead of the long and severe gradients to Shap and Beattock of its rival, the LNER had only a single short one, the 4¼ miles at 1 in 96 of Cockburnspath bank in Berwickshire, against southbound trains.

It was a route which, in pre-grouping days, had brought a remarkable degree of unanimity in locomotive design among its constituents. The Great Northern, owning the first 160 miles to Shaftholme Junction, north of Doncaster, and with running powers thence into York, had developed into a 4-4-2 railway under H. A. Ivatt for its heaviest and fastest passenger trains. On the North Eastern, which owned the next 175 miles to Berwick-on-Tweed, Vincent Raven also regarded the 4-4-2 as the most suitable machine for its trunk passenger work. The North British, too, owning the last 58 miles into Edinburgh, had adopted the Atlantic arrangement for its heaviest express work, though not between Edinburgh and Berwick; they were content to afford running powers into Edinburgh to the North Eastern and leave them to provide the power, rather than be involved in more engine changing.

The later GNR Atlantics were being built (and earlier ones rebuilt) with superheaters from 1910, turning them from undistinguished performers into outstanding engines for their size. Even as late as 1936 No 4404, standing station pilot at Grantham, had had to take over the 17-coach 13.20 Kings Cross–Edinburgh after the failure of an A3, and worked its 585 tons to York, 82.7 miles in 86½ minutes net. That wide firebox could be put to good use in producing horsepower, once the engine had managed to get the train on the move. Surely no North Eastern Atlantic could have put up such a showing.

So when Nigel Gresley took full charge at Doncaster late in 1911, his priorities had been not locomotives for the express passenger trains but engines to deal with the burgeoning freight traffic. For the first ten years of his superintendency all effort was devoted to building up this part of the fleet, with new classes of 0-6-0, 2-6-0 and 2-8-0 engines. They included the large K3 2-6-0s, with their 6ft diameter boilers and the three-cylinder O2 2-8-0s, highly capable machines which revolutionised the main line

Kings Cross station at (what appears to be from the clock), 10.55 in the late 1960s. The old barriers and signs are still in situ with stairs from central footbridge to all platforms. The scene is now altered completely with overhead wiring, new barriers and signs: the platforms have also been renumbered (8 is now 7). The trains today are mainly either electric multiple-units or Inter City 125 units.

Kings Cross main departure platform No 10 probably in the mid 1950s. The Heart of Midlothian *has just departed for Edinburgh while L1 Class 2-6-4T No 67774 stands in platform 8 with the empty stock for a later departure.*

69

express goods and mineral workings. Not until during and after World War I did the passenger situation change; train weights, if not speeds, were increasing, and engines with more pull at the drawbar and greater boiler power were needed.

Gresley, in particular, was a firm advocate of engines being right on top of the job, regarding it as quite wrong to build machines just big enough to work single-handed nine days out of ten but needing assistance under the heavier conditions of the tenth. Far better a big engine policy, even if a significant slice of their work could be done by something smaller; that made for reliability, greater scope for intensive working and (within limits) overall economy. He and Raven on the NE turned to the 4-6-2 arrangement in 1922. The Raven Pacifics were never satisfactory and had short and ineffective lives; the Gresley engines went from strength to strength.

By the time of Treacy's early interest in 1938, Gresley's policy had placed the East Coast route in the capable hands of no less than 114 Pacifics, the 4-6-2-2 rebuild of the high-pressure engine No 10000, and 44 Green Arrow 2-6-2s, with more building. Nor

Kings Cross station from the portal of Gas Works Tunnel with a 'Baby Deltic' No D5900 hauling empty stock from platform 12 and polluting the atmosphere. St Pancras station clock gives the time as 09.25 and the date is probably the mid 1960s. The LNER 'quad-art' stock is probably the most uncomfortable ever conceived, seating the maximum number of passengers in the minimum space, six a side with knees interlocked.

should we forget the six big 2-8-2s for the Aberdeen road and the pair of 2-8-2s built for the Peterborough mineral traffic. (By contrast, at this time the LMS was having to manage with just 28 Pacifics). Their size and good front ends enabled them to be driven on a fairly light rein, and under the diligent guidance of inspectors and their superiors, drivers were making the legendary 18 per cent cut-off working with wide-open regulator a well-nigh standard practice. Furthermore they had pushed speeds under test conditions from 100mph in 1934 to a maximum of 126mph in just four years. Running on the East Coast main line was very much in the public eye – and approval – with its streamlined services, and Treacy could not ignore them.

It was not Pacifics all the way, of course. In the London area the chunky-looking N2 0-6-2 tank engines were busy on stopping passenger and empty stock trains, their gruff bark linked to immense sure-footedness. On the lighter Cambridge expresses, B17 Sandringham 4-6-0s (the great rock-and-rollers of their day) shared duties with Ivatt Atlantics. On the freight lines to Ferme Park there were processions of Gresley K3s and 2-8-0s, with

Kings Cross main line station from Gas Works Tunnel showing Class 47 No D1871 in original two tone green livery leaving with 1A50, The Yorkshire Pullman, composed of the 1960 Metropolitan-Cammell cars. The locomotive is in pristine condition possibly for working a Royal train. There is a good view of York Road platform on the left, and the track into the tunnel towards the Metropolitan Widened Lines.

Kings Cross goods yard. One of Immingham's K3 Class 2-6-0s, No 61837, departing on a train of empty fish vans for Grimsby. Fish is one of many types of traffic which have completely disappeared from BR. In the 1950s there were daily fish trains from Aberdeen, Wyre Dock (Fleetwood), Hull and Grimsby to London and many other big cities.

A Class N2 0-6-2T hauls a main line empty stock train from Kings Cross to Bounds Green past Belle Isle signalbox. The North London line crosses the bridge in centre of the picture and the lines on the right lead to Kings Cross Goods and Top Shed. The signalbox on the right is 'Goods and Mineral Station'.

Green Arrows now in charge of the more important jobs such as the afternoon Kings Cross – Niddrie fitted freight. Other Gresley engines seldom appeared at the Cross, though they were often the mainstay of provincial services; one thinks of the Shires and Hunts in the Leeds/York/Newcastle area and in Scotland, the V1 and V3 2-6-2 tanks on various city networks, and the J38 and J39 0-6-0s in the northern industrial and mining areas and on country branches. Progressively his engines were cutting the ground from under the pre-grouping types.

In large measure Gresley's policies continued after his death in harness in 1941, though the short reign of Edward Thompson as CME made some dents in them. His B1 mixed traffic 4-6-0, however, simple machines in the mould of the Stanier Class 5s, carved out a niche for themselves on the medium-weight trains which Gresley had always declined to fill. His successor, A. H. Peppercorn, continued the Pacific tradition with two classes of post-war engines which combined many of the best features of Gresley and Stanier practice, and gained for themselves a high reputation for performance and availability.

In recording the scene, Treacy made his debut in the area of the five tunnels between Wood Green and Potters Bar. Here the lighter Coronation and Silver Jubilee trains could be making up to 70mph on the continuous rise at 1 in 200, the exhaust beat reduced to a purr, but with the heavy principal trains, loading to twice as many coaches, the pace was necessarily slower and the music at the chimney rather more 'forte'. Part of this section was no more than double track until the widening works of 1955, and the all-stations locals to Hatfield and beyond had to be sprightly with their trains of Quad-Art coaches to keep their paths between the expresses. This section must have witnessed some appalling struggles during the second world war, when trains of up to 25 coaches were commonplace, but Treacy was not around to record it, being away in the forces.

It was Kings Cross station that later took Treacy's photographic fancy, from the buffer ends to Gasworks Tunnel. The

Former War Department Austerity 2-8-0 (ER Class O7) No 90657 of Peterborough (New England, 35A) leaves Hadley Wood Tunnel with an up express freight probably from New England to Ferme Park or Kings Cross. The locomotive was built by the Vulcan Foundry of Newton-le-Willows, Lancashire in 1944 and was numbered WD 78715. It was lent to the LNER in November 1947 and taken into BR stock in December 1948. The photograph was probably taken in early BR days as the crossheads have not been modified to take LMS type gudgeon pins.

cramped throat area was always alive with activity – expresses arriving and departing, locals emerging from the suburban platforms or disappearing from the York Road platform down the 'drain' to Moorgate, light engine movements from the servicing depot alongside or from Kings Cross Top Shed. The whole was presided over by that tall, archaic-looking wooden signal box in the middle, imposing its will by colour-light signals surmounted by rattling roller blind route indicators. What sinuous paths the trains took in getting from the platforms on the York Road side to the fast lines, and what opportunities for slipping on greasy rails through the pointwork and in the smoky depths of the tunnel. So bad could it be in there, scrambling up the 1 in 107 after a shaky start, that lights were fixed at intervals on the tunnel walls so that drivers could know whether they were still moving forward! From perches above the tunnel mouth, and at rail level, Treacy recorded it all. Diesels here did not attract him for long. The Class 47s when new created a passing interest, but seemingly only the Deltics came anywhere near taking the place of the Gresley Pacifics.

Then there was the other popular spot nearby – the short four-track open section between Gasworks and Copenhagen Tunnels, including Belle Isle box controlling the entrance connections to Kings Cross Goods Yard and Top Shed. With down trains pounding up the hill, speeds were low and smoke plumes near-vertical. The slightly uneven exhaust beat of a Gresley Pacific – very thin and rasping when fitted with double Kylchap blastpipes – mingled with the more 'Jazzy' beat of Green Arrows. A picture could be conjured up at almost any time from engines ringing off the shed, or waiting a path down into the Cross, to supplement the central theme of dragging trains on to the easier grades through Finsbury Park.

Treacy dallied briefly with Peterborough (its imposing bridges on the southern approach offered him some scope), Grantham and Doncaster, but rightly described it as 'scarcely the most exciting bit of railway line in England'. Doncaster, however, was the junction point for trains to his beloved Leeds Central; here was a cramped main line terminal which he freely described as 'scruffy', approached over heavy grades, in marked contrast to the water-level entrances of the Midland into Leeds, and with excellent vantage points and semaphore signalling tailor-made to Treacy's style. On the main East Coast route, however, he could not get excited until York, where every train, be it proud streamlined passenger or humble freight, crept slowly through the station or on the goods lines round by York Yard. The vast station roof was a thing of beauty in itself, contrasting with the blackened massiveness of Holgate bridge, while in the background the Minster distanced itself from such things temporal. At the north end, the main and Scarborough lines diverged

Deltic No D9006 The Fife & Forfar Yeomanry *heads 1A50,* The Yorkshire Pullman, *passing Hadley Wood station after the opening of a second tunnel and quadrupling of the line. Date is the mid 1960s as the locomotive is still in two tone green and leading van is crimson lake.*

The solitary Class W1 4-6-4 No 10000 leaves Potters Bar tunnel on the 16.00 down express to Leeds and Cleethorpes in 1938.

No 10000 was originally built as a high pressure four-cylinder compound with Yarrow water tube boiler in 1929 and rebuilt as a three-cylinder simple, in this style in 1937. Nameplates Pegasus *were actually cast for No 10000 but never fitted.*

An Ivatt Atlantic as LNER Class C1 4-4-2 No 4417, heads a Cambridge to Kings Cross buffet car express near Potters Bar. The date is the late 1930s.

sharply in a welter of point and crossing work, making a most difficult start for heavy trains already in the grip of the platform curve. Starting was not helped by Gresley's practice of restricting maximum cut-off to about 65 per cent, and slipping was often heavy and ill-controlled. To stop blind involved drivers in a tiring performance of reversing with the heavy vertical screw, much blowing from open cylinder cocks, and often a stiff regulator making fine control impossible. It could be a masterly picture of steam and smoke, and a positive cacophony of noise until the train was finally on the move, but by no stretch of the imagination could it be regarded as good operating.

But undoubtedly, on the East Coast line proper, it was the two northern city stations, Newcastle and Edinburgh Waverley, which gave Treacy the greatest pleasure. Not only could he photograph trains both in the stations and on their approaches, but the very buildings themselves – no architectural masterpieces internally – lent themselves to the portrayal of delightful and cathedral-like patterns of sunlight penetrating the gloom and heavy shadow. Indeed, he was not averse to the odd picture using this feature with no train in sight. These stations stand as memorials to the Victorian steam era, and are increasingly incongruous in the age of diesel traction and, in the future,

78

electrification. Both stations also offered adjacent features which could be incorporated into the picture to its great benefit.

Newcastle was approached from the south by the four-track King Edward Bridge high above the industrial Tyne, with sharply curved approaches at each end and the Durham/Northumberland boundary sign in the centre. At the other end the road/rail High Level Bridge brought the coast line in, overlooked by the stone keep tower of the 12th century castle. The major divergences at each end gave rise to uniquely concentrated patterns of diamond crossings, a matrix on which to base the train picture. Until 1955/6 the whole was straddled by massive semaphore signal gantries of amazing complexity, a nightmare to read in the dark. Through this scene clattered a stream of passenger trains, hauled by almost anything from Pacifics on the main line down to V1s and V3s on Hexham locals, and electric multiple-units to the coast, while the freight running round the river side of the station could bring a mixture of V2s, NER 0-8-0s of both two and three-cylinder types, B16s and 0-6-0s. There were no gradients to speak of, but everything picked a delicate path over the difficult trackwork at sedate speeds. In the 124 miles on to Edinburgh, Treacy dabbled only briefly around Berwick, on Cockburnspath bank, and at Portobello. Even the Royal Border Bridge over the

Peterborough Crescent Junction, just south of the station, before the remodelling of the layout to permit 100mph running on the through roads. Class 47 No D1509 hauls a down express of BR Mark 1 stock all in maroon livery. The date is about 1963 or 1964.

79

Tweed – which is not at the border but two miles south of it – gave him little opportunity.

But Edinburgh Waverley was very different from Newcastle in its setting. It lay in a straight valley between the Calton Tunnels to the east and the Mound Tunnel on the west. The whole area was overlooked on the south side by the tall buildings of the Old Town, rising up to Edinburgh Castle on its rocky plinth. On the other flank was Princes Street, the outer development of the Georgian New Town, dominated at the Waverley end by Calton Hill. As befitted a city basking in the title of 'the Athens of the North', the Hill was topped by the observatory and the columned (and never finished) National Monument to the victory at Waterloo, in Greek temple style. The North British Hotel pile, its clock tower ever set two minutes fast for the benefit of belated passengers, brooded over the station itself, while above the Mound Tunnel were the classical buildings of the Royal Scottish Academy and the National Gallery. High over the station roofs strode the arches of the North Bridge linking Old and New Towns. What a photogenic setting for a railway! The locomotive

Peterborough North station looking north with the Great Northern Hotel in the background, in the mid 1960s. All this has been swept away and a brand new station has taken its place. The train in the platform (1E10) is the 11.34 from Bradford to Kings Cross.

The solitary Class W1 4-6-4, now renumbered as 60700, with an up express approaching Stoke near Grantham around 1952, after the first repaint in dark green. The stock is the 1948 Flying Scotsman train in BR crimson and cream livery.

depots were tucked away at a decent distance a mile-and-a-half on each side, St Margarets to the east (now the area is given over to a multi-storey office block and green lawns, to the relief of local residents) and Haymarket westwards.

There was nothing very uniquely Scottish about the trains by the time that Treacy made their acquaintance. There were still a few North British engines about, usually unkempt and not very imposing. The massive Atlantics were long gone. No longer did the Waverley pulsate with the throb of Westinghouse air brake pumps. Gresley and his successors ruled supreme. In the 1950s Haymarket turned out A1s, A3s and A4s for the London workings, their tenders piled high with Scottish coal, and made strenuous efforts to ensure that they were clean and polished to be a credit to the 64B shedplate. The same could seldom be said of St

Two GNR/LNER Class O2 three cylinder 2-8-0s coming off Grantham shed, (35B) both fully coaled. The locomotive nearest the camera is No 63935 one of the batch built at Doncaster in 1923/4 with GN cabs as Class O2/12. It was rebuilt in April 1958 to Class O2/14 and fitted with side window cabs. The other locomotive is also from this batch but retains the small cab although it now has an LNER standard tender. No 63935 has tablet exchange apparatus for use on the single line High Dyke branch at Colsterworth Mines. This line served ironstone quarries and was the reason for these locomotives being stationed at Grantham.

Margarets, whose grimy engines performed a high proportion of freight work from Niddrie, Portobello, Meadows and Seafield yards, and latterly from the new Millerhill. Treacy concentrated mainly on the east end of Waverley, his stances either above the Calton Tunnels, at rail level or perched on signal platforms. At the north end his preferred spots were in Princes Street Gardens, beyond the Mound, where impressively smoky exits from the tunnel were to be had for the waiting. With dieselisation, his style tended to change. The Deltics, clean and shining as they stood in the gloom beneath the station roof, became the new objects of his attention; their engines screamed at their fast idling speed, and as they started, much slower than other types because of a proneness for the amps to surge and bring out the circuit breakers, they would emit a cloud of blue/grey lubricating oil smoke which died away only slowly.

Treacy ventured no further north than the nine miles to South Queensferry and the instantly recognisable Forth Bridge, opened in 1890. Even then it was the form of the bridge rather than the trains on it which impressed him; it was very difficult to combine the two effectively. It was its setting astride the Firth of Forth, with the busy vehicle ferries *Queen Margaret*, *Robert the Bruce*, and the others shuttling back and forth which claimed his camera.

An up express, possibly from Newcastle, hauled by Class 47 No D1528 leaving Doncaster. Although the whole area was controlled by colour-light signals and two signalboxes, it has since been resignalled and Doncaster power box now covers an area from south of Grantham to north of Shaftholme Junction plus branches. There is still some steam in evidence outside the 'Plant' and there is no blue and grey stock so the year must be 1963 or 1964.

Doncaster with a down express headed by Class 47 No D1526. St James' church on the left was built for the use of GNR staff and paid for by subscriptions from GN Shareholders and friends. It was consecrated in October 1858.

View from the footplate of a Class A4 4-6-2 leaving Wakefield Westgate on an up train. The up starter is a single-aspect searchlight colour-light signal and the junction signal for the connecting spur to Kirkgate (former L&Y station) can be seen on the viaduct.

Facing page top:
Class 47 No D1543 heads a short Kings Cross to Leeds train passing Ardsley station in about 1965 (closed 31 October 1964). Presumably a Bradford portion was detached at Wakefield. In the background is the coaling plant of Ardsley locomotive shed.

Right:
The prototype Birmingham Railway Carriage & Wagon Compnay diesel-electric locomotive No D0260 Lion on the up Yorkshire Pullman leaving the 297yd Ardsley Tunnel between Leeds and Wakefield in September 1963. Lion, built in 1962, was not adopted by BR due to the doubtful financial position of BRCW and was scrapped in 1965. It was on loan to the Eastern Region only briefly from the beginning of September to October 1963. Eric Treacy photographed it at least three times in this short period.

Beeston Junction, Leeds on 21 May 1948 during the nationwide locomotive exchanges, showing Great Western Railway King Class 4-6-0 No 6018 King Henry VI hauling the 07.50 Leeds to Kings Cross. Due to clearance problems, the Kings Cross to Leeds route was the only non GWR line over which the King could be tested. The leading vehicle is the ex North Eastern Railway dynamometer car now preserved in the National Collection at York. The branch to the right was to Hunslet GNR goods depot. In the 'V' is an example of the LNER's efforts to tidy up the lineside with concrete edges, raked chippings and shrubs.

Leeds Central with another Class 47, No D1514, about to depart at the head of an express formed partly of LMS stock, about 1965.

The building behind the station is the Great Northern Hotel which is still in business although renamed the Wellesley, after Arthur, first Duke of Wellington (it is in Wellington Street). The station was closed on 29 April 1967 and has since been demolished.

A local train in the Leeds area: ex GNR Class C12 4-4-2T No 7353 passes Copley Hill on a three-coach train about 1950. Its destination is Wakefield direct or via Tingley & Batley. The locomotive was renumbered to BR 67353 in April 1951 so the photograph is before that date but after 1949 as it carries a BR shed plate, 37B Copley Hill, as well as the stencilled name on the buffer beam. The stock is all LNER, a brake third and an articulated pair consisting of a lavatory composite and a brake third. The old LNWR line out of Leeds is to the right and at a lower level.

Leeds City, east end, with *The North Briton* (Leeds to Glasgow) about to leave hauled by LNER Class A3 4-6-2 No 60084 Trigo. *The coaches are all ex LNER and the picture is dated as 1951.*

On the next road is ex NER Class D20 4-4-0 (NER Class R) No 62373 of Starbeck shed waiting to back onto its train to Harrogate via Wetherby.

The scene from Holgate Bridge (possibly taken with the aid of an orange box, steps or a kitchen chair!) with two freight trains coming off the goods lines avoiding York station.

On the left is Class O4/5 2-8-0 No 63851 of Frodingham, a War Department locomotive built after the end of World War I in 1919, and purchased by the LNER in 1924. It was rebuilt with a Gresley round top boiler in 1939. The train is probably bound for Scunthorpe. The right hand train is hauled by Class B16/3 4-6-0 No 61464. The date is the mid-1950s.

There was still plenty of cattle traffic judging from the number of wagons in the dock on the left. Behind the trains are the various buildings of York South locomotive shed closed in 1961 and demolished in 1963.

York station, south end, in the mid-1950s. A Class A1 4-6-2 lurks in the shadows on platform 8 while LMS Class 5 4-6-0 No 44776 of Saltley (Birmingham) is about to leave from platform 3 with a local to Sheffield. Class J71 0-6-0T No 68250 is south end pilot and is shunting a BR Mark I corridor brake third. The NER headquarters offices can just be seen peeping over the city walls.

A down East Coast express passing York station on the through road hauled by Class 55 Deltic No D9016 before being named. Although the station is basically the same today, there are many detail differences. The track layout has been simplified and signals removed, the station lighting has been modernised and most important of all the roof and buildings have been cleaned and repainted.

Facing page, bottom:
Class K3 2-6-0 No 61940 of Doncaster leaving York, platform 1, on an express to Doncaster in 1957. Standing on the up through road between platforms 8 and 9 is Class D49 4-4-0 No 62737 The York & Ainsty.

The north end of York station with a down express (1N48) 11.42 Lincoln–Newcastle, made up of a mixed collction of Thompson and BR Mark I stock with a TPO bringing up the rear. The connection from platform 14, 15 & 16 and the goods lines to the Scarborough line appears to have been lifted. The lines from platforms 12 & 13 are still in situ but probably disused. (The former NER head office opened in 1906 is prominent in the left centre background).

An anonymous wartime scene possibly on the East Coast Main Line north of Northallerton, with a very grimy Class D49/2 4-4-0 No 362 The Goathland very unusually hauling an up express freight. The middle portion of the train consists of cattle wagons, but one suspects that they were being used to carry vegetables or similar inanimate objects rather than livestock. The stencilled shed name on the buffer beam is not quite readable but looks like Tweedmouth.

King Edward Bridge, Gateshead, over the River Tyne from the County Durham side. Class A2/3 4-6-2 No 60500 Edward Thompson *hauls a mixture of Gresley, Thompson and BR Mark I stock on an up express. The large building to the left of the bridge on the Newcastle bank is Forth goods depot now demolished.*

The Gateshead end of King Edward Bridge with Class A3 4-6-2 No 60036 Colombo *hauling the up Queen of Scots Pullman. No 60036 would work as far as Leeds Central where the train reversed. The smokebox door is badly burned from an accumulation of ash: the LNER arrangement of the door closing onto asbestos rope packing was never a good one to prevent air leakage but this has excelled itself.*

A view of Gateshead from the footplate of a Class A1 Pacific crossing King Edward Bridge over the River Tyne. The Bishop must have been leaning right out of the cab and holding his camera at arms length to obtain this shot.

The Anglo–Scottish border sign at Marshall Meadows about three miles north of Berwick. These signs were erected between the wars at all the points where lines crossed the border. The original signs were removed for 'security reasons' in 1939 and were replaced by this BR design after nationalisation.

Cockburnspath Bank, Berwickshire, with an up freight hauled by Class V2 2-6-2 No 60806 (of Heaton shed, 52B). A case of carrying coals to Newcastle!

Portobello Junction near Edinburgh (the junction for the Waverley route) with Class A3 4-6-2 No 60091 Captain Cuttle heading an up East Coast Main Line express about 1957.

The main lines were later slewed to ease the curves following the closure of Portobello station seen in the background. Much of the siding area on the right is now the Edinburgh Freightliner Terminal while Craigentinny HST Maintenance Depot is on land to the left released by slewing of the main line.

The east end of Edinburgh Waverley station taken from above Calton Tunnel with a Class 40 English Electric diesel heading the up Talisman. The North Bridge is straddling the station and the old town is on the left of the picture with the Castle in middle distance. This picture shows the relatively low roof of Waverley, which was restricted to 42ft by the Scottish law of 'Servitudes' equivalent of 'Ancient Lights' in England.

Edinburgh Waverley showing east end pilot, Class J83 0-6-0T No 68474 of St Margaret's in the early 1950s. Although a plain black engine, it was kept in good condition with embellishments on the smokebox. St Andrew's House, the Scottish Office is behind the locomotive.

Edinburgh Waverley with Class J37 0-6-0
No 64622 emerging from Calton Tunnel
with a down coal train in the early 1950s.

An up Edinburgh–Kings Cross express
leaving Waverley hauled by Class A4 No
60010 Dominion of Canada *and about to
plunge into Calton Tunnel. The tender is
overfull with coal and approximately 2ft
above cab roof, and the quality looks very
dubious for a long run. From the direction
of the sun the train is probably either The
Elizabethan or The Flying Scotsman.*

Class B1 4-6-0 No 61308 (St Margarets, 64A) with an up local train leaving Waverley station about 1958. The time on the North British Hotel clock is 11.30.

Edinburgh Waverley station, east end, with Class A2 No 60530 Sayajirao on the up Queen of Scots, a surprisingly grubby turnout for a Haymarket Pacific on an important train.

Light and shade at Waverley station, Edinburgh, showing the southerly main line through platform with a small queue waiting to be admitted. Like the majority of Scottish Region stations, Waverley is now 'open' without platform barriers.

Edinburgh Waverley station, showing the northerly main line through platform No 19. An up express from Aberdeen has just arrived and the date is sometime in the early 1960s.

The west end of Edinburgh Waverley station with Class V2 2-6-2 No 60835 The Green Howard (Heaton, 52B) leaving platform 11 probably for Glasgow Queen Street.

The Mound Tunnel, Edinburgh, from one of the footbridges in Princes Street Gardens, with Class 47 No D1760 on a Glasgow Queen Street train in the late 1960s.

The down North Briton leaving the Mound Tunnel, Edinburgh, hauled by Class A3 4-6-2 No 60090 Grand Parade (Haymarket, 64B). The photograph is dated between August 1958 when Grand Parade was fitted with a double chimney and January 1963 when it received trough type smoke deflectors.

Haymarket, Edinburgh, with Class V1
2-6-2T No 67610 (Haymarket, 64B)
passing the locomotive shed with a down
stopping train, possibly to Hyndland via
Queen Street low level. The date is the
mid 1950s.

The Forth Bridge from South Queensferry
landing. At the slip is the pleasure vessel
The Second Snark, now on the Clyde, and
one of the four ferries is approaching. The
ferry services ceased in 1964 with the
opening of the Forth Road Bridge.

BR Standard Class 5 4-6-0 No 73152, fitted with Caprotti valve gear and hailing from St Rollox, 65B, crosses the Forth Bridge with an up local which is mostly of LNER stock. Access to the pathways adjoining the tracks was available by means of a special walking permit. It was the practice of passengers, for many years, to attempt to throw old style pennies into the water: most failed and there was a rich harvest for the stretch ganger.

Driver in cab of a Gresley Pacific. The driver's name and his depot are not known. The regulator is wide open and he has his hands on the vertical screw reverse.

THE MIDLAND ROUTE

The Midland? To the North? Surely not; the Midland went to the English Midlands – places like Leicester, Nottingham and Derby. One might be tempted to go to St Pancras for Manchester, and probably for Sheffield. But the north? No, for that one went to Euston or Kings Cross, depending on one's destination.

There was more than a grain of truth in these simplistic misconceptions. After all, the original constituents of the Midland Railway ran from Rugby or Hampton-in-Arden (for which the starting point had to be Euston) and finished up in York or Leeds (where one transferred to other companies to get to Scotland). It was not until 1857 that the Midland managed to reach the English capital independently of the LNWR, and only then by courtesy of the Great Northern from Hitchin into Kings Cross; only in 1868 did it finally get its own St Pancras terminus. Likewise, at the other end of the system any traffic for Scotland had to be given to others. Its first attempt to get further north ended at Ingleton, and even when the LNWR connected that moorland town to the West Coast main line at Low Gill in 1861, there was so much obstruction that virtually no through passenger traffic chose to go that way.

The Midland main lines paraded their varied parentage and piecemeal construction for all to see. North from St Pancras it was for the most part a very fast road, apart from the slowings for Wellingborough, Market Harborough and Wigston, where the sweeping curve joined the old Midland Counties line from Rugby. Onward, things went well until the Erewash Valley, north of Toton, where in later years mining subsidence turned the foundation into a rolling sea. It pressed on to Leeds in high-handed fashion, using the low ground and ignoring such places as Sheffield, Barnsley and Wakefield save by branch lines. The alignment was good and gradients modest, but again man ruined its quality by subsidence on a widespread scale. From Leeds it meandered up Airedale to Skipton and fizzled out in the by-ways of the 'Little' North Western. Hardly a 'route north' here.

If the LNWR had been more accommodating for Midland traffic north of Ingleton, that might easily have been the end of the story – useful if one lived in parts of Yorkshire and the Midlands for getting northwards, but not exactly a major traffic artery. Five years of obstruction, however, finally led the Midland to seek powers for its own line to Carlisle to by-pass the LNW

St Pancras station in the early 1970s. Class 45 No 79 heads an express at platform 3. The scene is very different today with most of the expresses formed of Inter-City 125 sets. However, Barlow's magnificent roof and Scott's Hotel remain and are listed buildings.

completely. What is more, the Settle & Carlisle line was built under great difficulties of terrain and at very high cost, as a fast main line; this involved very heavy tunnelling and bridgework in remote areas. But the Midland accorded it the necessary priority in its spending plans, considering it justified to be able to carve its own slice of Anglo-Scottish traffic; the Midland entered into arrangements with the Glasgow & South Western to haul its trains through Nithsdale to the Clyde, and with the North British to do likewise through the Border country to Edinburgh via the Waverley route, opened in 1862 (14 years before the Settle line).

The Settle & Carlisle line was a fascinating piece of railway. Whereas the LNWR got through the fell country without a tunnel (it had none on the main line north of Shugborough) the Midland needed no less than 13 between Settle and Carlisle. Twelve major viaducts had to be built to keep gradients reasonably even and

110

alignment good. The summit point in the Pennines, Ais Gill at 1,169ft, was over 250ft higher than the West Coast route at Shap Summit. The weather could be atrocious, with high winds which regularly whipped tarpaulins off wagons, and with heavy drifting snow. Magnificent in summer, it could be a nightmare during the winter months. In spite of all it became truly a trunk route to the north, albeit perhaps the most difficult to operate and always with a time penalty of about an hour for through passengers compared with the West Coast route. Its main impact was in providing services to suit Midlands passengers for Scotland and largely left the southerners to its two rivals.

In this passenger field, the Midland philosophy of running light trains at frequent intervals, rather than assembling the big caravans of coaches of some of its competitors, complemented the operating view that there was no necessity for any engines bigger than 4-4-0s. Crewe must have been amazed, and slightly contemptuous, to see the load limits rigorously imposed over the Settle & Carlisle, as well as elsewhere. The biggest engines built specially for the line, the 990 class (similar in size to the Compounds but two-cylinder simples) of which there were but ten, were allowed to take no more than 230 tons, this at a time

Jubilee Class 4-6-0 No 45626 Seychelles leaves Derby with a Newcastle to Bristol express about 1950. The stock is all ex LNER and most is still in varnished teak livery. The locomotive looks very clean and is probably just out of shops; it is, in fact, a Derby engine. The platform on the left was originally used for ticket collection in connection with MR trains off the West of England line and no doubt LNW and NS trains too. The wheel has now gone full circle and Derby is again an 'open' station.

LMS Class 4F 0-6-0 No 44420 of Derby shed on a train of coal empties on the Ripley branch near Derby in the early 1950s. The locomotive is freshly painted after a general overhaul at Derby works and has a tablet exchange apparatus on the tender no doubt for workings over the M&GN. The road on the left is the A61 from Derby to Leeds and Thirsk.

Class 45 No D27 heads train number 1V39, the up Devonian, 10.36 Bradford to Paignton at Oakenshaw North Junction. The track trailing in from the right is the ¾ mile long goods only connection to the former L&Y Wakefield to Goole line, opened by the LMS on 3 June 1928. Although the signalbox is of MR design it was installed by the LMS as there is no mention of it in the 1922 Appendix to the Working Timetable.

when on the West Coast the broadly similar-sized George the Fifth 4-4-0s were regularly taking half as much again and more over Shap. The smaller Class 3 Belpaires and Class 2 4-4-0s took correspondingly lower tonnages, with the result that even in normal times there was a marked degree of piloting; at holiday periods with strengthened trains it tended to become the rule rather than the exception.

On the freight side, traffic flows southwards from the Nottinghamshire coalfield were very heavy, and Toton Yard in particular assembled a stream of heavy mineral trains for the London area and the West which were well beyond the capacity of even the latest Class 4 0-6-0s. So it was the normal practice for Class 4 and Class 3 0-6-0s to be assisted, usually by other 0-6-0s, but at times of stress by almost anything else, even such diverse and unsuitable machines as 4-2-2 singles and Tilbury 4-6-4 tanks!

In general, locomotive provision during the first seven years of the LMS did little to rectify this nonsense. There was a limited transfer of LNWR Claughton 4-6-0s to the Midland in the last

A mystery train on the approach to Leeds hauled by Class 40 No D276. The coaches are nearly all LNER non-gangwayed suburban and cross-country stock which form a load for a crew-training special. The signalbox in the background, Wortley North, controls the NER line from Harrogate. As there is no yellow warning panel on the locomotive, the date must be 1959.

years of the decade, but they were an unknown factor to Midland men and did little to relieve the position until Patriots could be allocated in some numbers from 1932. The building of the Garratts in 1927/30 was supposed to be the answer for the Toton–Brent coal trains, since they could take 1,300 tons and more, but they proved to be far from satisfactory as a result of incorporating (at LMS insistence and against the practice of the builders) outdated design features derived from the Class 4F 0-6-0s and other pre-grouping locomotives. Small numbers of Fowler 0-8-0s (the Austin Sevens) were allocated at the same time, which proved highly efficient on 900 ton trains but suffered from mechanical weaknesses common to the Garratts. It was not until the mid-1930s that Stanier was able to make a major impact on Midland Division motive power with the influx of large numbers of Jubilees, Class 5s and (a little later) Class 8F 2-8-0s, making possible the introduction of important accelerations in the passenger services and the takeover of the main mineral flows from the obsolescent 0-6-0s.

This was the railway scene which met Treacy when he returned from the forces in 1945 and resumed the civilian ministry in Keighley. The Midland south of Leeds seemed to interest him little, surprisingly, perhaps, for there was no shortage of locations similar to those he used on the East Coast line a few miles away. But the Welsh Harp goods line flyover, the tunnel portals at Elstree, Ampthill and Red Hill, the deep cuttings at Sharnbrook and the winding curves of Chiltern Green apparently went unnoticed. Things started at Leeds City, and it was from there, on a gradually diminishing scale with increasing latitude, that he toted his camera.

Over the Settle & Carlisle, apart from the staple diet of Jubilees, Class 5s and 2-8-0s, four classes of locomotive will always be specially remembered. Taking them in order of appearance on this route, the first were the rebuilt Royal Scots in 1943. Right from 'new', a number of them were based at Holbeck shed for the expresses, and put up some remarkable performances on the 1 in 100 slogs to Blea Moor and Ais Gill. Their steaming was irreproachable and they could really pile on the power. Rough-riding they could be at high mileages, with an accompaniment of savage grinding noises as the trailing wheel tyres rubbed on the firebox expansion angles, but enginemen were prepared to put up with that if the engine performed. Treacy rode on their footplates and appreciated their capabilities as they tackled the long climbs noisily on 30 per cent cut-off and wide-open regulator, and got rid of incandescent small coal at the double chimney.

Next (in 1948) came an allocation to Holbeck of Class 5s with Caprotti valve gear, brand new engines, fitted with all mod cons and intended to be the last word. But they immediately showed

Leeds City Midland side with rebuilt Royal Scot No 46117 Welsh Guardsman of Holbeck shed, 20A, leaving on the down Thames–Clyde Express. There is no doubt about the year, 1953, as Welsh Guardsman carries one of the special Coronation headboards. The train is made up of a mixture of BR Mark I and LMS stock.

114

The up Thames – Clyde express leaving Leeds City (MR side, formerly called Wellington) hauled by Class 5 4-6-0 No 44746 with Caprotti valve gear, of Holbeck shed. The 20 Caprotti Class 5s were not popular on the Settle & Carlisle line, being weak on the banks. This one has been modified with straight outside steam pipes instead of the original curved pattern, and it shows!

themselves to be the wrong engine for working over the Settle & Carlisle, their Caprotti gear making them weak on the banks compared with the otherwise identical piston valve engines. Oh, they could coast extremely freely *down* the hills, but they made heavy weather of getting up them first. As far as possible they were drafted to work in other directions.

Relief for the hard-pressed 2-8-0s appeared in 1954/5 with the use of the new Standard Class 9F 2-10-0s on the 'Long Drag' freights. These were really just what was needed under the difficult conditions of the line, powerful, with ample boiler power for sustained climbing, sure-footed, free running at speed and above all, comfortable. They were remarkable in giving no impression of speed on the footplate, being very smooth riding and quite devoid of axlebox knock. Also used on the Water Orton–Carlisle fitteds were the three of the class fitted with mechanical stokers and allocated to Saltley, though the stokers were not a howling success (at least partly due to the difficulty in getting suitable coal on to the tender).

116

Finally, in the last years of steam, came half-a-dozen A3 Pacifics. Now these engines were more in the nature of racehorses than suitable for heavy pulling at low speeds on long banks; they were not brilliant on the Waverley route, for instance, and could soon become embarrassingly short of steam and water. But the simple modification of fitting double Kylchap exhausts, which were applied to all the A3s from 1959 onwards, changed them out of all recognition. They became very much at home on the Settle line, and were popular with the LMS-orientated crews.

The line northwards out of Leeds City was, for Treacy, God-sent; apart from the passenger activity at the west end of the station itself, where there were not only the Midland trains but also the Newcastle–Liverpools over the ex-LNWR route, there was the Midland triangle based on Engine Shed and Whitehall Junctions. Everything was pulling hard as trains leaned to the curves at low speeds, and for icing on the cake there was a proliferation of Midland lower-quadrant and standard upper-quadrant signals. All was grist to Treacy's mill. Through this small area pounded the Carlisle expresses, behind Royal Scots, Jubilees, Class 5s, Britannias and (for a very few years) A3s. On the locals, Compounds worked out their last days alongside 2-6-4 tanks and others. No lack of variety troubled the photographer. And if there were quiet moments, it was no great distance to slip down into Holbeck shed, where there was always suitable material on tap.

Leeds Whitehall Junction, with a Class 4P Compound 4-4-0 No 41081 from Lancaster heading a Leeds to Heysham parcels train in the mid 1950s. The lines off to the right are those of the MR to St Pancras, and behind is the beginning of the LNW 'new' viaduct. The engine has a strengthened front frame section to counter the weakness of the original shallow section which always buckled under anything but modest impact.

A mile up the line was Holbeck Low Level, where the ex-L&Y and GN lines crossed over on impressive bridgework. Here, not only were the Leeds City trains beginning to gather speed but they were joined by trains out of Leeds Central for Harrogate and points north. This way came the prestigious Queen of Scots Pullman for Glasgow; an A3 or V2 job. Before the closure of Leeds Central, the Holbeck stations were cleared away, improving the landscape of the area substantially.

From there until reaching the fell country Treacy used his camera sparingly, at locations such as Keighley, Skipton, with its over-generous six-platform station (and the possibility of trains being diverted via the Ilkley line if there was a blockage on the main) and the attractive Midland stations at Gargrave and Bell Busk. Hellifield, another imposing junction station, out of all proportion to the village it served as a sort of afterthought, also saw him occasionally, though at this distance from Leeds the service was becoming a little sparse.

It was the climbs to the Pennine summits, however, with which he found himself most in harmony. The line pursued its lonely course in this bleak countryside against most impressive skylines, dominated by the distinctive outlines of Pen-y-Ghent, Ingleborough, Whernside and Mallerstang Edge, all around 2,300ft or more. The line gently curved round hillsides, leaped over valleys on impressive viaducts, and regularly dived into tunnels under the fell. The passenger trains hammered up the 1 in 100 grades at 30–40mph and then scuttled across the tableland at 60 or more. It was all material for Treacy's camera, perhaps nowhere more so than in the vicinity of Dent station, 1,150ft up and reached by a steep track from the minor road up Dentdale. Two miles further north, beyond Rise Hill Tunnel, lay Hawes troughs, the highest in the world. They were never short of water, but it was all too common for them to freeze in winter. Then down to Appleby and on through wooded country to Carlisle. It was on Appleby station, in 1978, that Eric Treacy collapsed and died. It was a great loss to the enthusiast ranks, but how fitting that it should have been beside the line which, above all, had given him immense pleasure.

North from Carlisle the Midland expresses used the Sou' West's Nithsdale route to Glasgow, some 13½ miles longer than the Caley line and involving some hard but relatively short slogging climbs. Treacy almost totally ignored it – not because it lacked attractive locations to suit his style, but probably because it was off his beaten track. Some pleasant but by no means exceptional pictures at Dumfries, both at the south end by the motive power shed and, at the north, at the junction of the Stranraer line, seem to be all that he took.

The trains to Edinburgh via the Waverley route received rather more of his attention. There were distinct similarities with the

Holbeck Low Level about 1960 with Britannia Class 4-6-2 No 70054 Dornoch Firth *on the down Thames–Clyde Express. This was the last Britannia to be built and is attached to a 4,725 gallon tender. There appears to be a bad leak on the left hand clackbox and the engine is blowing off. The Midland signalbox on the left is Wortley Junction.*

118

One of the now preserved Jubilee Class, 4-6-0 No 45593 Kolhapur backs down into Bradford Forster Square station in 1966. Note the exceedingly long footbridge which crosses all the approach tracks and the goods yard.

The locomotive appears not to have any lining but is still green, no doubt an economy at the end of the steam era when the accountants who ruled BR resented every penny spent on steam locomotives. The yellow band on the cab indicated locomotives which were prohibited under the wires south of Crewe. The nameplate, a painted version written after the original cast brass ones had been removed, shows an incorrect spelling – Kholapur. The shed plate 55A is Holbeck, Leeds under the new BR numbering code.

Settle & Carlisle; a ten-mile pull from Newcastleton, mainly at 1 in 75, took the line over Whitrope summit at over 1,000ft, passing on the way the isolated outpost and community of Riccarton Junction. Riccarton was entirely inaccessible by road, and the local shed ran a train into Hawick each Sunday to take the residents to church. After that 12-mile drop into Hawick on gradients little easier, and over a broken profile onwards to Galashiels, trains were faced with the second major bank, 15 miles of it and mainly at 1 in 100/150, to get over the Moorfoot hills at Falahill summit, at nearly 850ft. From the Edinburgh side it was much worse, with nearly 10 miles almost continuously at 1 in 70 from Hardengreen Junction (where the Peebles line parted company) up to Falahill. Not only were the gradients punishing but curvature was incessant. The Waverley route joined the East Coast main line at Portobello East Junction, 3½ miles east of Edinburgh Waverley, where the signalbox sat on an overhead structure straddling the running lines and trembled with every train passing under it.

The Waverley route in postwar years sustained a limited passenger service between Edinburgh and Carlisle, calling at most stations, together with two through trains to and from St Pancras, the Waverley by day and an overnight train with sleeping cars. Even the latter train seemed to emphasise the provincial nature of the Midland by declining to book sleeper berths from Edinburgh further than Nottingham! In addition there was a heavy freight traffic, mostly in fully or partly fitted trains, from Aberdeen, Perth and the Edinburgh area to Carlisle yards for the LM Region. On such a road, unbraked wagons were a serious liability! In North British days the principal trains had been in the hands of the massive Reid Atlantics, a design chosen perhaps more for the flexibility of its wheelbase on this curvaceous road than for the suitability of four coupled wheels on such gradients. The lesser trains were handled by Scott and other 4-4-0s and the big J37s worked the freight. But by the time that Treacy got to know the line it was almost totally Gresley-ised. A3s, mostly from Carlisle Canal shed worked most of the passenger turns and some of the fitted freights, which otherwise were in the hands of travel-stained V2s, B1s and K3s from St Margarets. It was one of the early stamping grounds of Haymarket's Class 26 and Class 40 diesels when they first arrived.

The Midland Railway terminus in Bradford, Forster Square with Kolhapur *on a parcels train. The chimney lamp bracket has been moved to the side of the smokebox to reduce danger when under the new electric 25kv overhead wires. The warehouse in the background has painted thereon 'Railway Goods and Wool Warehouse' indicating Bradford's staple trade. The present station replaced Market Street on 2 March 1890 and is now very much run down, being used only by diesel multiple unit trains to Keighley and Ilkley.*

Skipton station from the north with Stanier Class 4 2-6-4T No 42442 on a local train, probably for Colne, in platform 4. Platforms 5 and 6 to the right were added later when the line to Ilkley and the Yorkshire Dales Railway to Grassington were opened.

A view from the footplate of Class A3 4-6-2 No 60081 Shotover *heading a Leeds to Glasgow train passing Keighley in about 1960. The double chimney, fitted to* Shotover *in October 1958, improved the steaming of these engines for hard climbing as on the Settle & Carlisle road. Keighley Station Junction signalbox and the connection to the Worth Valley branch can be seen through the bridge.*

Much of the southern end of the line was relatively inaccessible to photographers, and Treacy seems to have started at Whitrope box, a lonely spot in a blind valley from which the line escaped by diving into Whitrope Tunnel, whence it emerged in the tight and winding glen carved by the Slitrig Water. Below Shankend station the line swept over an attractive viaduct; it was reverse curves all the way as it came down past Stobs into the knitwear capital of Hawick, its station on a curve high over the Teviot river. Here was always something to see – trains being shunted, the Whitrope bank engines preparing for their next job, the odd terminating local to be disposed of.

Galashiels, the next important station and famous for its woollens, was set tight with the town and the tumbling Gala Water as they jockeyed for position in the narrow valley bottom, under the gaze of stone house terraces on the hillsides. But by the time the wriggling line had reached Falahill the countryside had opened out completely, the box and goods loops sitting in the middle of pleasant grazing country. Soon one was into the Lothian coalfield and the pit bings of Arniston, Lady Victoria and many other collieries now mostly defunct, passing the 1961 Millerhill Yard (now at the end of spurs from the East Coast main) and into Auld Reekie herself. It was a very hard and expensive line to work, and the delightful scenery could not keep it open; closure came early in 1969. But Treacy was in time to sample it during its postwar best, and has brought out much of its character.

Snaygill, near Skipton, 220 miles from St Pancras with rebuilt Royal Scot Class 4-6-0 No 6108 Seaforth Highlander of Holbeck shed hauling an up express in 1947. The engine is in the 1946 livery but without smoke deflectors. No headboards are visible nor is there a restaurant car in the train so it may be a relief.

The up Thames–Clyde Express passing Skipton South Junction hauled by Britannia Class 4-6-2 No 70054 Dornoch Firth. The engine, allocated to Holbeck, looks neglected and the right hand cylinder cover casing is missing.

The signals behind the first coach are LMS upper quadrant arms on Midland posts and are unusually tall for MR signals to enable them to be seen over the road bridge.

Two Jubilee Class 4-6-0s head the down Waverley near Gargrave in the late 1950s. The train engine appears to be priming badly which may account for an assistant engine on only nine coaches. However, No 45691 Orion, (an Upperby engine) shows signs of drawing air through the smokebox door so it may be a case of two lame ducks!

The down Thames–Clyde Express passing Gargrave with Britannia Class 4-6-2 No 70053 Moray Firth in charge around 1960. The last batch of five Britannias were originally allocated to Polmadie (Glasgow), hence the names of Scottish Firths, but when this photograph was taken No 70053 was at Leeds Holbeck no doubt displaced from the West Coast main line by Class 40 diesels.

*Bell Busk near Hellifield with No 70053
Moray Firth again, this time on the down
Waverley.*

*Ribblehead Quarry with Jubilee Class
4-6-0 No 45691 Orion of Kingmoor shed
(12A) passing on a down freight probably
in the early 1960s.*
  *If the Settle & Carlisle line is closed
this will be the railhead for the remaining
southern section from Settle Junction.*

*Ribblehead station in 1959 with a down
express hauled by Class A3 4-6-2 No
60036 Colombo. The train is probably
the down Waverley as it appears to
consist of only 10 coaches and the
restaurant car is an ex LNER vehicle.*

Ribblehead viaduct and not a soul in sight. This structure is now giving cause for concern and may bring about the closure of the Settle to Carlisle line. Even when this photograph was taken, the second arch from right was under inspection – note the scaffolding.

Ribblehead viaduct in typical Settle–Carlisle weather. A Class 5 4-6-0 is tackling the 'long drag' from Settle Junction to Blea Moor Tunnel hauling a partially fitted freight.

Approaching Dent station, the down Thames–Clyde Express is hauled by Britannia Pacific No 70053 Moray Firth. The year must be 1957 as the stock is all crimson lake but the engine still carries the first BR emblem. Dent was the highest main line station in Britain, 1,150ft above sea level. The viaduct in the background is Arten Gill.

129

The up Thames–Clyde Express approaches Ais Gill summit, passing milepost 260 – another 20 chains to go – hauled by Class A3 4-6-2 No 60082 Neil Gow of Holbeck in 1960.

Facing page, top:
Dent station, with an up local leaving. From the direction of the sun, it is probably the return 'Boniface' from Hawes to Bradford Forster Square. Note the double snow fence on left.

Facing page, bottom:
The famous stockaded turntable at Garsdale (or Hawes Junction as it was known) used to turn the pilot engines which had assisted up trains from Carlisle. The story that an engine was whirled round and round by a high wind is probably pure myth. The stockade was built to protect engines from the wind and make it possible to turn them against the very high velocity gales encountered there.

A LMS Hughes/Fowler 'Crab' Class 5 2-6-0 No 42864 (Agecroft, 26B) heads an up freight on the last ½-mile or so to Ais Gill summit. The date could be any time between 1951 and the early 1960s; there is no clue at all in the picture. Ais Gill up distant is towards the rear of the train. The fire irons are badly stored on the tender and look most unsafe – a feature of the Fowler 3,500 gallon tender.

Class 45 No 15 approaches Ais Gill on the up Thames–Clyde Express (1M86) sometime in the late 1960s. This is difficult to date accurately and thus the originating terminus could have been Glasgow St Enoch (closed July 1966) or Glasgow Central.

An up freight (reporting No 8E01) approaches Ais Gill with Wild Boar Fell in background. The locomotive is an unidentified Class 45 and the date uncertain but again probably the late 1960s.

Class 25 No 5235 on a down freight, reporting No 8M18, near Ais Gill around 1970. Although only a Class 8 train the majority of the wagons appear to be vacuum brake fitted. The locomotive appears to be in two tone green livery but the D prefix has been dropped.

The up Waverley crossing Dent Head viaduct hauled by a Class 45 diesel electric locomotive about 1965. Dent Head signalbox can be seen in the middle distance. The locomotive is painted in the two tone green livery with a small yellow warning panel.

The Eden Valley near Armathwaite with the up Thames–Clyde Express hauled by two Jubilee Class 4-6-0s which are tackling the climb to Ais Gill. The pilot is No 45729 *Furious* but the train engine is unidentifiable.

Facing page:
Carlisle Citadel station during the rebuilding of the roof in 1957. The overall roof which covered the tracks to the right of the picture has already been removed and work is progressing on the portion over the main platform. Jubilee Class 4-6-0 No 45694 *Bellerophon* of Leeds Holbeck shed stands at the down platform with *The Waverley* from St Pancras to Edinburgh (Waverley).

Carlisle Citadel station, north end, about 1958 after the rebuilding of the station roof and resignalling. Class A2/3 No 60519 *Honeyway* is just departing on the down Waverley. The original electric lighting on the engine has been removed but it retains the stovepipe double chimney. The north end station pilot, LMS Class 3F 0-6-0T No 47354 is standing on the middle road.

The up Waverley passing Durran Hill Junction signalbox in the late 1950s hauled by Jubilee Class 4-6-0 No 45728 Defiance. The stock is composed of seven BR Mark I coaches and an LMS restaurant car. The signalbox dates from the 1890s and is unusual for the Midland as it is 15ft from front to rear. The North Eastern line to Newcastle passes behind the box.

Carlisle Citadel station, north end, with Class A3 4-6-2 No 99 Call Boy probably waiting to take over a Waverley line express off the Midland. The photograph was taken between February 1947 when No 99 was renumbered from 2795 and July 1949 when it was repainted BR blue and renumbered 60099.

Class J39 0-6-0 No 64964 of Carlisle Canal shed leaves the Caley main line for the North British line on the 17.08 local to Langholm composed of three LMS corridor coaches. A spring time shot in the early 1950s.

Riddings Junction, on the Waverley route, with a Langholm branch train in the bay platform behind Class J39 0-6-0 No 64943 probably in the early to mid 1950s. This type of railway scene, the country junction, has now vanished for all time though it was an integral part of the railway for well over a hundred years. The single coach and two vans could hardly be called an economic load and it is surprising that the service lasted until 15 June 1964. The branch signal is in the off position ready for the shunt and locomotive run round.

The up Thames–Clyde Express approaches Dumfries No 1 signalbox double-headed by LMS Class 2P 4-4-0 No 40665 and Royal Scot No 46109 Royal Engineer. The Hurlford Class 2 will no doubt come off at Dumfries having assisted the heavy train from Kilmarnock. A Class 5 4-6-0 is waiting on the down Stranraer line before setting back into the station.

Dumfries (former Glasgow & South Western Railway) with a local to Kilmarnock and Glasgow just leaving the station hauled by Class 5 4-6-0 No 45010. The area appears to be in the throes of resignalling as none of the signal posts have any arms attached but the replacements are out of sight of the camera.

The former Caledonian branch to Lockerbie curves away in the middle left of the picture.

Facing page, top:
Former Caledonian Railway Mackintosh 0-6-0 No 57609 heads a train of coal empties up a colliery branch, probably in Ayrshire in the early 1950s. Many of the wagons are wooden ones of 12 tons capacity requisitioned in 1939 and never returned to their owners.

Facing page, bottom:
Weather problems further south seem to be anticipated as the double-headed up Thames Clyde Express leaves Kilmarnock behind Class 5 4-6-0 No 45432 (fitted with a snow plough) and an unknown rebuilt Royal Scot Class 4-6-0 around 1957. This was an unusual Treacy location.

Ballochmyle viaduct on the former Glasgow & South Western Railway with a BR Class 5 4-6-0 heading a down 10 coach train of LMS stock. Ballochmyle is the largest masonry arch and the highest railway bridge in Britain, with the central span over the River Ayr covering 181ft; it is 169ft above the river bed.

140

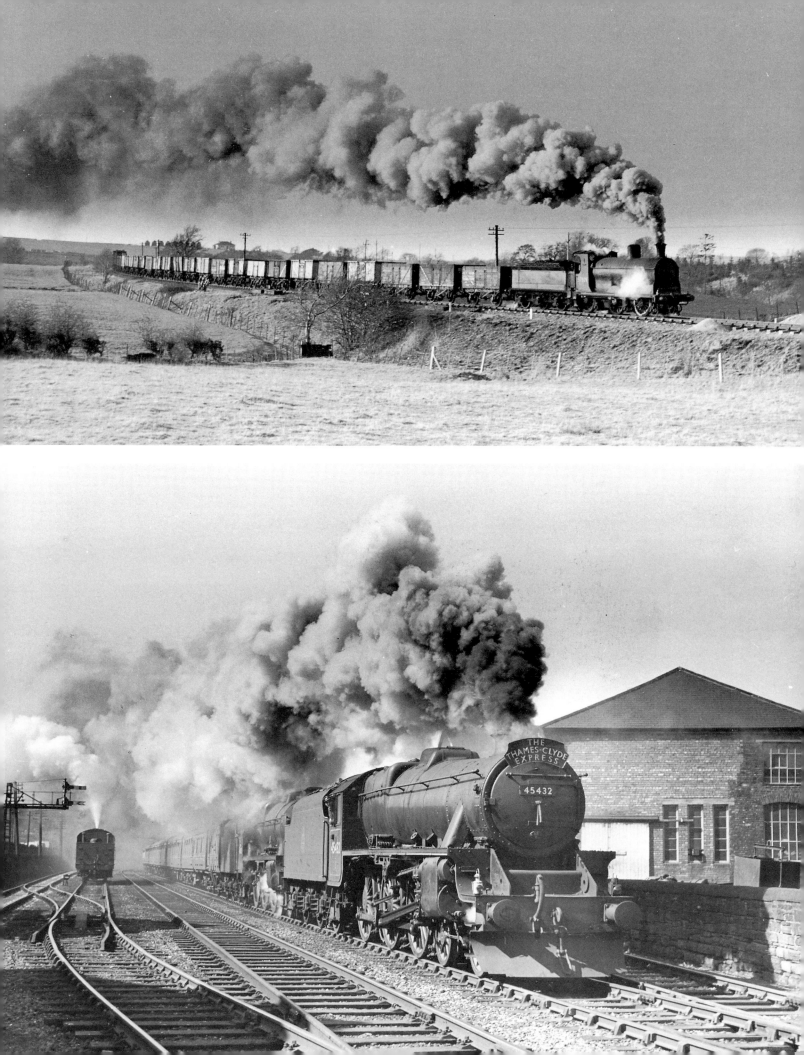

The Waverley route at Whitrope
signalbox looking towards Edinburgh
Whitrope was at the summit of a 10 mile
climb from Newcastleton (down) and 11
mile climb from Hawick (up). Just beyond
the signalbox the line plunged into
Whitrope Tunnel under a ridge 1,300ft
above sea level.

Shankend viaduct with Shankend
station in the background. Class A3 4-6-2
No 60093 Coronach heads a down
express just starting away from Shankend
station about 1957. Even the stopping
trains often carried express headlamps
over this route.

A parcels train approaching Shankend on the Waverley route headed by B1 4-6-0 No 61219 (64B Haymarket) banked in the rear from Hawick to Whitrope. In the late 1950s and early 1960s the Waverley route carried considerable through freight traffic between eastern Scotland and the LM Region almost all in fully or partially fitted trains. These were never very heavy because of the long and severe grades.

The up Waverley from Edinburgh to St Pancras above Stobs station climbing the 1 in 80 to Whitrope summit hauled by Class A3 4-6-2 No 60093 Coronach about 1958. The A3s did not take kindly to the heavy pounding on the Waverley route in single chimney days. The climb up the valley of Slitrig water was severely curved.

Running under ex North British Railway signals Class B1 4-6-0 No 61290 of 68E shed (Carlisle Canal) takes a through freight into Stobs station, south of Hawick in the early 1960s. Note the single van traffic to the left of the picture, a facility now long withdrawn, also the neatly kept flower beds and the rotating shunt signal for the goods bay.

Hawick station with Class K3 2-6-0 No 61968 hauling an up partially fitted freight. A Class J36 waits behind the platform to bank the train to Whitrope. The entrance to the engine shed is on the left with a Class C15 4-4-2 tank lying dead on the siding.

Galashiels station with an up parcels and freight train headed by Class B1 4-6-0 No 61191 sometime in the early to mid 1950s. The road bridge across the station is still there today but now there is no trace of any railway – track, buildings or ballast.

144

Falahill signalbox, the main northern summit of the Waverley route with an unidentified Class K3 heading a down fitted freight. Another K3 is just appearing round the corner on an up train.

Another view of Falahill with an up local approaching behind Class B1 4-6-0 No 61308 from an unidentifiable shed but still carrying the name on the buffer beam as well as a cast shed plate: it is probably St Margarets, Edinburgh. Upper quadrant arms are fitted to the old NBR lattice signal posts. The train is either an Edinburgh to Hawick all stations or possibly running through to Carlisle. The former is the most likely as through trains usually carried express headlamps although stopping everywhere. Note the sash cord windows on the front of the signalbox.

NORTH-WEST TO THE HEBRIDES

To Englishmen the Highlands and Islands of Scotland have a certain fascination, even though surprisingly few of them have ever been there. Gaunt mountains, rocky coasts and bays of purest sand, rushing burns and tranquil lochs, afforested hillsides, the air of spaciousness, and the inevitability of ferrying across water are all ingredients. So, too, are the gentle pace of life and the sense of timelessness and peace. So in some ways the presence of a railway is an anachronism, a searcher for traffic flows where few exist, a disciplined and clock-geared organisation in a land where, apart from pubs and post offices, time is governed as much by the light as by man-made devices.

It was invariably difficult country through which to project a railway, and the limited traffic potential ensured that it was built and operated as cheaply as ingenuity could manage. Single track was unquestioned (though the Highland Railway did subsequently double certain critical sections of its line), gradients were severe, with 1 in 60 commonplace, and curves tight and unceasing. Often viaducts looked disproportionate to the streams beneath them – until one saw those same streams in spate after storms, rushing peaty-brown torrents moving rocks and trees before them. The stations tended to be mere crossing loops, a siding, perhaps a level crossing, and a nucleus of wooden buildings surrounded by a clump of trees for shelter and little else but moorland. There was a very real sense of struggle, against the terrain, the climate, everything. The infrequent train service made each arrival, and especially those bringing newspapers and the post from the south, an event worthy of a reception committee. The train represented the outside world, and what it carried, be it human or material, was of interest to those whose lives were rigidly circumscribed by their environment.

For visitors from the south – and that includes everyone from Scottish Lowlands to the English Channel – there were three railway gateways to this enchanting land. First in the field was Perth (or more strictly speaking, Stanley Junction, seven miles north) from where the Highland Railway completed a single line of rails to Inverness in 1863 and reached the sea at Strome Ferry, on Loch Carron, in 1870. The final section from there to Kyle of Lochalsh had to wait another 27 years for completion. It was a very roundabout route, for a Glaswegian making for Skye was faced with 289 miles of rail travel – more than twice what the

Perth station main line platforms in the early 1970s. Two Class 26 diesels, No 5331 as pilot plus another unidentified locomotive, head an Inverness to Glasgow train. The station by this time has been resignalled. On the right, behind the station wall, is the unloading dock for Motorail Cartic 4s.

crow required – and this was only shortened to 263 miles by the opening of the cut-off line from Aviemore via Carr Bridge in 1898.

The next in the field was the Caledonian, with the Callander & Oban line in 1880. Oban, however, was much further south, and the line served only the southern fringe of the Highland massif, while Oban's steamer services were mainly directed to Mull and the southern islands of the Hebrides.

It was understandable that other interests should seek ways of tapping the tourist, fishery and agricultural traffics of the western seaboard. The West Highland Railway, a protégé of the North British, found a much shorter way to Skye, opening its line from Craigendoran Junction, 22 miles west from Glasgow along the north shore of the Clyde, to Fort William in 1894, and then further to Mallaig in 1901. This brought our Glaswegian a short steamer trip from Skye at the end of a 164 mile train journey, a substantial saving in time and fare.

Treacy first directed his camera to the Highland line during the 1950s. By this time Highland locomotives had all but disappeared. The prime passenger engines, Cumming's Clan 4-6-0s, had gone by 1950, having been transferred to the Oban line when new Class 5s were drafted to Perth and Inverness in 1934. Only two of the ill-fated River class 4-6-0s, which after being rejected by the Highland in 1915 and banished to the Caledonian, had returned during the 1920s, survived the second world war. The Highland locomotive stud had been sacrificed on the altar of the Stanier Class 5. Only the doughty little Cumming 4-6-0 Superheater Goods engines remained on their rightful work, handling the trains on the Kyle road, passenger and freight alike. But the writing was on the wall; the replacement of the Kyle turntable, enabling Class 5s to be turned, bounced them off these jobs, and after pottering about for a year or two the last of them went to the torch in 1952. Only months later, the little 4-4-0 *Ben Alder* was set aside, hopefully for preservation; after some years it was evident that this was not to be (how bonny she would have looked at Bo'ness) and she went to her Valhalla. Henceforward the Class 5s – including the BR Standard version – had it almost to themselves. Until, that is, the arrival of Class 25, 26 and 27

Aviemore, ex Highland Railway, with two Class 25 diesels Nos D5120 and 5115 on a down Inverness train in the early 1970s. Both locomotives are blue but D5120 has not yet lost its prefix and has two powerful headlights for the Far North lines. There are signs of the development of Aviemore as a resort with the new building dominating the right background.

Class 26 No D5331 on an up Kyle of Lochalsh to Inverness train entering Strathcarron station 46 miles from Dingwall (the mile post can be seen opposite the points). The train is composed of 100 per cent LMS passenger stock plus what looks like a Great Western meat van (telegraphic code MICA) next to the engine.

This scene which was taken about the mid 1960s is completely different now as the A890 road crosses the line here and parallels it along the southern shore of Loch Carron through new avalanche shelters. At this time, the road went along the north shore and vehicles crossed the loch at Strome Ferry.

diesels, which promptly took over the services, sometimes in pairs and with help from other classes.

Treacy's photography here in the 1950s seems to have been concentrated on the Kyle line itself; not for him the attractive locations in Strath Tay and the Pass of Killiecrankie with its turreted viaduct. Perhaps he judged it as suffering from overexposure already. Nor did he haunt the lonely summit at Druimuachdar, itself at 1,484ft and flanked by 3,000ft mountains, nor the impressive viaducts over the Findhorn at Tomatin or the Nairn at Culloden Moor. Even on the Kyle line his locations were limited and seemingly governed by convenience of access at stations. He did not record the splendid sight of a Class

5 pounding up the 1 in 50 to the summit of Raven Rock on 50 per cent cut-off, nor its meanderings along the wooded rim of Loch Garve. Nor did it occur to him to bring out the economical tablet working, where often the tablets were exchanged at the station buildings (where the token instruments were located) while points and signals were controlled from small signalboxes, little more than ground frames, at each end of the loop. Signalmen quickly work-studied the walking movements involved. But he could not fail to rise to the delights of Kyle station, approached past the small stone shed and through a rocky cutting containing the signalbox, its island platform and buildings set on the pier end-on to the sea. Over the buffer stops and you were in the water. As its backcloth were the mountains of Skye across the narrow sound, and particularly in the light of a summer evening the scene could look quite magical. How many people besides Treacy must have travelled the line for the sole purpose of savouring this small and isolated village.

There is no indication that Treacy ever knew the Oban line, save where it passed below the West Highland at Crianlarich. Its southern end, from Callander to Crianlarich, was to fall to the Beeching axe in 1965, but nature preferred to pre-empt that by a landslide a few weeks earlier; better that way than mildly accepting decisions from distant powers. After that Oban was reached via the West Highland.

Overleaf:
The end of the line. Kyle of Lochalsh terminus showing a Dingwall and Inverness train about to leave behind Class 5 4-6-0 No 45179. The ex Highland island platform station has hardly changed since pre-grouping days and neither has the general scene apart from the modern Macbrayne's coastal ferry Loch Seaforth *and the 1950s motor coach. The scene is overshadowed by the 'Dark Isle' – the Island of Skye, across the Sound of Sleat.*

Below:
Kyle of Lochalsh from the bridge over the station about 1953 showing ex Caledonian 0-4-4T No 55216 shunting and an LMS Class 5 4-6-0 leaving on an Inverness train. Note the cattle van and pens on the left of the picture showing a form of traffic now lost to the railway completely. Either the freight train guard or a shunter is reading his paper on the footplate of the 0-4-4T.

The West Highland line had an aura quite different from that of the others. Perhaps the attractive style of most station buildings on its island platforms had something to do with it. Perhaps it sprang from the contrast between the rural cleanliness of the line itself and its grimy preliminary passage through the sandstone tenements and industry of the Glasgow suburbs. The demarcation came after Dumbarton, and at Craigendoran Junction the West Highland hived off from the coast line at 1 in 58 to become a true Highland railway. It skirted lengthy lochs, climbed fiercely to three major and separate summits (the highest, at Corrour, at 1,350ft), picked its way across the desolate Rannoch Moor, and kept close company with the River Spean in the Monessie Gorge before reaching Loch Linnhe and Fort William. Here, the station that Treacy knew, on the loch shore by the steamer pier, has gone, replaced in recent years by a new combined railway and bus station which shortens the rail journey by a few hundred yards.

If the Fort William line impresses, the Mallaig extension had a more gentle air. Fierce gradients there certainly were, steeper indeed than before Fort William, but they were shorter. The line kept closer company with the sea and its beaches of silvery sand, and seemed a more integral part of the tiny communities that it served. Did not the curved Glenfinnan Viaduct – an early example of the use of mass concrete – stand cheek by jowl with the monument to Bonnie Prince Charlie? And so to Mallaig, a fishing port and very little else, once a major source of traffic for the line; alas, no more.

During the second world war, with military training and preparations for invasion in full swing in the Highlands, the whole territory north of the Great Glen became a restricted area, thus affecting passenger traffic beyond Fort William. During this period it was discovered that ingenuity had found means of breaching the bonded stores of the Talisker distillery on Skye, and it was thought that some of the precious malt whisky was being helped to travel south via Mallaig, courtesy of certain railwaymen. One evening, therefore, a small bunch of customs men with a railway officer arrived at Mallaig Junction signalbox after the last train from Mallaig had left the previous crossing point, and instructed the signalman to stop the train. As it came to a stand and the reception party emerged from behind the box, the driver quickly disappeared from the cab window of his K2 2-6-0, and before he reappeared there was a sudden flash of blue light from the firehole. Asked what had caused it, he ruefully replied, 'Ach, it must ha' been the speerit o' ma' ancestors!' Needless to say, no evidence of whisky movement was discovered that night. It would have been difficult, because in such a small, close-knit community everybody knew everyone else.

Tradition died hard on the West Highland. In the 1950s, when a new stationmaster was to be appointed to a station on the

Mallaig line, the interviewing panel decided that a certain individual was the most suitable for the post, only to be forced to change its mind at the last moment when it was realised that his name was Campbell and he would be totally, unacceptable in Macdonald country. Memories of Glencoe were too recent.

West Highland men were proud characters of sturdy independence; one had only to watch the accomplished hand-over-hand exchange of single line tablets at speeds well in excess of that ordained by authority to know that, and the philosophical resignation on the rare occasions when the pickup was missed and the train ground to a halt for the fireman to go back and find it.

If the Highland Railway had taken the early lead in using 4-6-0s on its lines, no such ideas sprang from Cowlairs. The pregrouping engines which will always be associated with the West Highland were the 4-4-0 Glens, which though not built specifically with this line in mind, nonetheless took it over from the original West Highland Bogies (later Class D35). These tough mixed-traffic engines, built from 1913 and superheated, were allowed to take 180 tons over these fearsome grades, and did much of the passenger work in pairs for 20 years; even after they were displaced several remained for piloting duties. But the gradual increase in passenger train weights meant that six-coupled wheels had to come, and it was Gresley who adjudged that his ex-Great Northern two-cylinder K2 2-6-0s were the machines for the job. They proved able to take 220 tons unassisted; but even that, representing five coaches plus a tail of fish vans, was too much, and piloting continued. Gresley then purpose-built the three-cylinder Class K4 2-6-0s for the line. This was a real case of 'multum in parvo', with nearly 33,000 lb of tractive effort in an all-up weight of 68.4 tons. They did some magnificent work, but the design proved something of a 'too much in parvo' for their mechanical health and in the post-war years they were pushed on to less arduous duties. First came the new Class K1 two-cylinder 2-6-0s, competent engines which hammered away at the long grades on 45 per cent cut-off without the pressure gauge flinching. They in turn gave way to the nominally less powerful Stanier Class 5s, the comparable BR Standard version, and Thompson's Class B1s. The whole line reverted to a four-beat railway after Gresley's three-cylinder interlude.

Treacy took no photographs at some of the most splendid locations on the line. He did not clamber up to Glen Douglas box, perched high above Loch Long, to await the twin pillars of smoke and healthy beat of engines fighting their way up the 1 in 57 from Arrochar, nor wait by the main road as the heavy afternoon passenger from Glasgow pounded up Glen Falloch. His most spectacular pictures were taken near Mallaig Junction as south-bound trains pulled out of Fort William, all smoke and noise, as

An up West Highland train near the Horseshoe curve headed by Class 26 No 5343 which is fitted with a small snow plough. The seven coach train including a buffet car is in blue and grey livery but the locomotive appears to be green which dates the photograph as late 1960s or possibly 1970.

Fort William with Class K4 2-6-0 No 61996 Lord of the Isles (Fort William on buffer beam) leaving for Glasgow on a partially fitted freight around 1952/53. This Class of six three-cylinder 2-6-0s was built specially for the West Highland line between 1937 and 1939. One was rebuilt as a two cylinder locomotive and Classified K1 and the remaining five were withdrawn at the end of 1961.

Class K4 three cylinder 2-6-0 No 61996 Lord of the Isles works south of Fort William probably in the summer of 1953 (The K4s were transferred to Eastfield in May 1954). The wagons at the rear of the train are empty bulk aluminium hoppers from the British Aluminium Company's smelting plant at Fort William.

Facing page, top:
Fort William with Class K1/1 2-6-0 No 61997 MacCailin Mor (the rebuild from Class K4) leaves Fort William with an up express to Glasgow (Queen Street) about 1952. The train is passing the goods yard where Class K2 2-6-0 No 61787 Loch Laidon and a J36 0-6-0 are standing. There will be a full restaurant car service on this train.

Facing page, bottom:
Fort William in the early 1950s with Class J36 0-6-0 No 65313 (Fort William, 63D) shunting; the locomotive shed is in the background. A total of 168 locomotives of this Class was built between 1888 and 1900 and they were used all over the NBR. It was a very long lived Class and the last examples were not withdrawn until 1967.

they fought for speed before the rising grades to Spean Bridge.

But steam did not last much longer. Doctor Diesel was at its heels, in the shape of Class 26s and 27s, and in 1962 these virtually ousted steam from the West Highland. Treacy watched them growl their way up to the 1,024ft summit between Tyndrum and Bridge of Orchy, but somehow the photographs lack the sense of all-out struggle which came out so clearly with their coal-fired predecessors. Now, they in turn have given way to the more reliable Class 37s. But still the West Highland proudly exhibits its individuality, in the shape of the little West Highland Terrier logo borne by Eastfield's locomotives working the line.

Class J36 0-6-0 No 65313 the Fort William pilot stands tender to tender with unnamed Class K2 2-6-0 No 61784 which is heading a short Mallaig freight, probably in 1952.

The 5.45 am train from Glasgow, Queen Street, (the overnight sleeping car express from London, Kings Cross) approaches Fort William terminus one day in 1952; it is double-headed by two dirty engines whose numbers are unidentifiable, a B1 and a K2. The K2 is the assisting engine working to normal West Highland practice when the train engine is in front giving the driver control of the brake. Waiting to back down to it, and to take the Mallaig coaches forward, is Class K1/1 2-6-0, probably No 61997 MacCailin Mor. Note the later upper quadrant arm to the home signal while the bracket signal retains its NBR lower quadrant arms.

A down Fort William to Mallaig train at Banavie Bridge over the Caledonian Canal about 1953. The beginning of the flight of locks known as 'Neptune's Staircase' can be seen on the left. The engine is Class K1 2-6-0 No 62031 built by the North British Locomotive Co in 1949.

Class K2 2-6-0 No 61790 Loch Lomond with side window cab for the West Highland line heads an up express along the shore of Loch Eil in the early 1950s. The visible stock is all ex LNER in the first BR livery. The second coach is a restaurant car so the train is probably the 13.00 ex Mallaig.

ON SHED

As befitted one who proclaimed his hobby to be 'pottering about locomotive sheds' – a barely adequate description of his railway interests – Eric Treacy spent a lot of time in them. But they were a demanding subject from which to obtain good photographs.

'Shed'; it is a strange word in the English language to use to describe a complex of activities in the service of locomotives. It is evocative more, perhaps, of the simple wooden erection at the bottom of the garden housing nothing more valuable than the lawnmower. The dictionary defines the word as a 'one-storeyed building for storing goods or vehicles or keeping cattle etc or for use as workshop etc and consisting of roof with some or all or no sides open'. In the railway context it was prefixed by 'engine' or (more grandly) 'locomotive', or 'steam' or (in the later and more diverse context of dieselisation, ('motive power'), thus distinguishing it from those used for carriages, goods, trains (in a US application) or even weaving. But it was far more than a roof over a walled or wall-less structure, for it encompassed everything which lay on the path between entrance and exit points. 'Depot' would have been much more appropriate as a description.

The functions of such an organisation were essentially to provide:
- a base for organising staff, with appropriate supervision;
- records of work done by engines and men for analysis and control;
- secure standage for locomotives not in traffic;
- coal, water, lubricants, sand etc to meet their working needs;
- means of disposal of their unwanted products of work, mainly ash, smokebox char and boiler sludge;
- facilities for their servicing and maintenance, including stores, within specified limits.

Such sheds could be of almost any size, from small outposts housing a single locomotive and with some functions carried out elsewhere, to vast depots with an allocation of 200 engines or more, and well over 1,500 staff.

Treacy's interest in engine sheds, aside from his parochial involvement at Edge Hill, was of course as an enthusiast seeking pictures, and as such he could afford to be highly selective. Particularly with straight sheds, with low roofs extensively obstructed by smoke troughing, and a total lack of open space, the light was usually so poor that effective photography was

A Class K2 2-6-0 rebuilt with side window cab and carrying a name working a train on the Mallaig extension. This scene is typical of the route with its many sharp curves and short rock cuttings. Everything is still totally LNER.

163

The south end of Camden (1B) with Princess Class 4-6-2 No 46203 Princess Margaret Rose taking water. All engines are facing north as Camden only served a terminal station. The photograph was taken in the summer as the steam heating pipe has been removed, and the date is the early 1950s. The shed was demolished in the mid 1960s and the site is now the holding sidings for coaching stock.

impossible except for longish exposures of static subjects, which was not really his style. The general standard of shed illumination – and gas was still in extensive use in the 1930s – was very poor, and the conditions of smoke, damp and corrosion further compromised its efficiency. So internally he confined himself almost entirely to sheds of the roundhouse type, of which the principal exponents were the Midland and the Great Western. Such sheds were usually much higher buildings, with large uninterrupted roof spans, windows in the side walls giving light in any position of the sun, and the large open turntable space in the centre enabling the camera to keep back from its necessarily large subject. In such lofty halls, atmosphere could be transferred to film as shafts of sunlight bored into the smoky air, just as it could in such favourite stations as York, Newcastle and Edinburgh Waverley. Working figures appeared in frozen silver-lined semi-silhouette as they went about their tasks. The angular shapes of steam locomotives were somehow changed in new patterns of light and shadow. So for Treacy the roundhouse, exemplified by

164

Crewe North (5A) in early BR days with Princess Class 4-6-2 No 46212 Duchess of Kent. The locomotive is in a temporary BR livery of lined black and still carries a domeless boiler. The old shed buildings were getting very tatty and were partially rebuilt a few years later. The shed was demolished in the mid 1960s and the site was cleared.

Crewe North (5A); the rebuilt section in the form of a semi-open roundhouse in the late 1950s. BR Britannia Class 4-6-2 No 70044 Earl Haig stands on the turntable of its home depot.

Edge Hill (8A), Liverpool, with rebuilt Scot No 46140 The King's Royal Rifle Corps (minus regimental badge) on the ashpits. The mechanical skip for disposing of ash into wagons is behind the locomotive. An Austerity 2-8-0 is dropping down from the goods loops onto the coaling stage. Edge Hill was a most complicated layout with lines going in all directions. This view shows the west end, the old shed, with goods lines leading to Wapping Tunnel behind the 2-8-0.

Holbeck (Leeds) and York (now ever more magnificent as the core of the National Railway Museum) were attractive places in which to 'potter about' with an eye to a stirring photograph.

But the 'shed' of the dictionary definition was but a part of the whole, and there was more of interest outside. In the 1930s both the LMS and LNE had spent a lot of money in updating the facilities at their larger and more important depots to speed the flow of engines through the servicing processes and make them available more quickly for their next work. Track layouts were modified to avoid conflicts, large mechanical coaling plants were installed which could fill a tender in a couple of minutes, and ashpits were modernised in several forms to handle the clinker, ash and smokebox char more easily and less labour-intensively from pit to wagon.

After 1954 no great changes were made before the great rundown to the end of steam in 1968 began. New construction was mainly confined to the BR Standard Class 9F 2-10-0s and Class 5MT 4-6-0s. A batch of 10 Britannias was split between Holyhead and Polmadie; in later years the Scottish engines were transferred to Holbeck and figured frequently in Treacy's pictures on the Settle & Carlisle. The 2-10-0s went in fair numbers to work Midland freight, including the Settle line for which they were eminently suitable, but also made a brief name for themselves in working summer express passenger trains on the East Coast route with speeds up to 90mph, remarkable for an engine with coupled wheels no more than 5ft in diameter.

Modernised or not, these areas were by no means the cleanest and most orderly in which to work. Dust flew, knobs of coal tumbled over the sides of full tenders, and any breakdown of ash handling plant quickly had the pit and its surroundings knee-deep in smouldering piles of clinker. Treacy undoubtedly savoured this scene, but curiously his pictures in this field seldom include man at his unpleasant labours, raking out ashpans and smokeboxes or trimming a bunker full of coal. Perhaps often a static, silent comment was sufficient.

The repair areas of sheds interested him greatly; it was, after all, worthy of attention, even a sort of sympathy, to see a locomotive standing minus a pair of wheels or stripped down for a valve and piston examination. Half-recognised chunks of machinery took on a new dimension when lying on the floor – a pair of springs, coupling rods, smokebox baffle screens. They looked different, if only (a sad reflection on conditions) because they had been cleaned. But again, surprisingly, it usually seemed to be the lunch-break when Treacy came on the scene. Perhaps working language was a little too robust!

Edge Hill was his introduction to this world of service to the steam locomotive. It was a fairly large depot, with about 115 engines of its own and acting as the district concentration depot

BR Class 6 4-6-2 No 72008 Clan Macleod of Carlisle Kingmoor (12A) in almost pristine condition. Someone has, however, already made a mess of the paint on the boiler cladding with a paraffin lamp, and the front buffer beam has received a bump.

166

Carlisle Kingmoor (12A) in the late 1950s with BR Class 6 4-6-2 No 72007 Clan Mackintosh at the south end of the shed building. The nearer water column appears to have a fire cresset hanging from the arm but if so, how is it brought down for attention – or was it filled with fire whilst in situ?

Facing page, top:
Carlisle Kingmoor (12A) probably in the early 1960s as the engines have electrification warning flashes. Class 9F 2-10-0 No 92015 has its rear ashpan side door hanging open and looks unkempt. The water columns with a balanced arm replacing the leather bag are an LMS design introduced about 1947.

Facing page, bottom:
Kings Cross, 'Top Shed' with Class A3 4-6-2 No 60108 Gay Crusader, Class A4 4-6-2 No 60017 Silver Fox and a BR Class 9F 2-10-0. No 60108 was fitted with a double chimney in June 1959 and received smoke deflectors in February 1962. The A4 is being prepared as there is a ladder alongside and the inspection door is open.

undertaking the bigger mileage examinations, etc, for about 290 engines in all. Basically a dead-ended straight shed, it nestled largely out of sight of the main lines in a pocket surrounded by high-level connecting lines to Edge Hill Yard. This feature was used by the LNWR to good effect when it installed a mechanical coaling plant and fed it at the top from a high-level loco coal wagon spur.

Of the sheds that Treacy made it his business to visit in later years, two stand out above all others. Kings Cross Top Shed was one of his favourite haunts when he could make the opportunity, and it was probably the continuous availability of Gresley Pacifics on view – home based or foreign – that made it so. Sooner or later just about every one of them came here, and there was often an impressive line-up, made more interesting, perhaps, by an A4 with its 'cod's mouth' open. A big shed, it was home to over 130 engines, of which some 22 were Pacifics and 11 V2s. These were the front-line elite troops, but nearly half its allocation was of the ubiquitous N2 0-6-2 tanks as well as the later L1 2-6-4 tanks, which between them virtually monopolised the suburban and

empty stock workings. Like many depots, it had its busy times and its slack ones; being a passenger depot, the night hours were fairly somnolent once the overnight sleeper trains had been powered, but it came to vibrant life as breakfast time approached, and in the mid-afternoon, as engines were prepared for the morning and teatime peaks. Another factor which endeared it to Treacy in the 1950s was the sustained effort to turn out its Pacifics in sparklingly clean condition.

Holbeck was undoubtedly the shed to which he devoted more time than any other. Of Midland parentage, it was bounded to the north by the ex-LNW direct line from Leeds City up to Farnley Junction and the west, on viaduct. No doubt many drivers of LNW upbringing looked down on it as something inferior, as LNW men would. There were bigger sheds, for it was home to just 93 engines, with the district contributing another 248; it had 18 Jubilees and 8 Royal Scots in 1954, and was the main provider of passenger power on the Midland route in both directions, for every train had to reverse in the Midland part of Leeds City station and be re-engined. On the freight side its 2-8-0s shared work with several other depots. Treacy did take some pictures in the shed yard, but it was the cathedral-like light patterns streaming in through the roof glazing and the high windows that attracted him and gave him the majority of his pictures.

His photographs at the other sheds which he visited suggest that he regarded them as very second-best. Camden he probably found an unsatisfactory substitute for Edge Hill; many of the engines were similar, and it was a cramped depot for its own allocation of 55 and for the many which worked in. It was so close to housing on one long side that there was a constant preoccupation with smoke prevention. With the inevitable post-war shortage of ground staff in the London area, its ashpits were ever poised on a knife-edge, and at times they nearly vanished under the torrent of clinker. Likewise Crewe North warranted few pictures; only its steel coaling plants, installed by the LNW and replaced after the second world war, were at all unique.

Of the other depots of which his photographs remain, it is sufficient perhaps to mention three. Kingmoor, two miles north of Carlisle, formed the background to many of his train pictures in the area. It was a very large but spacious depot, its engines working almost entirely into Scotland on passenger and freight (apart from a great deal of trip working between yards; much of this ended with the construction of the new and white-elephant Carlisle Yard). Yet the standard of maintenance of its engines was at rock bottom; the only criterion seemed to be whether they would run at all. On the other side of the country, Treacy's pictures of Gateshead were rather prosaic and lifeless. This was a proud depot, one of the last adherents on the East Coast route to

Kings Cross with Class A4 4-6-2 No 60028 Walter K. Whigham *under the coaling plant. There appears to be some trouble with the feeder chute of the plant which needs the fireman's attention as the coal on the tender is well above the cab roof. Perhaps he was trying to squeeze the last lump into the tender for the non-stop run to Edinburgh. Class V2 No 60936 stands behind wreathed in steam.*

Kings Cross with Class A4 4-6-2 No 60026 Miles Beevor *on the ashpit for disposal. The access doors to the smoke box are open but there is no sign of the oversize Allen key used for this operation.*

171

lodging turns (to London) but it comes over more as a flat and grimy wilderness. Across the border, St Margarets *was* a flat and grimy wilderness. It was a curious, cramped relic of earlier days. The East Coast main line ran through the middle between its two halves. The southern part was the more important, though on a very restricted site, and dealt with the main line locomotives. Its coaling plant was an elderly manual stage. It was surrounded on two sides by roads and housing, and smoke complaints were continuous. On the north side of the main line, in a vee with the Abbeyhill loop line, was the old part of the shed, where in the distant past new locomotives had been constructed. Now it was confined largely to the stabling of small engines and shunting 'pugs'. The two parts were joined by a walkway crossing, a potential death-trap as main-line trains thundered by; train-operated warning signs had to be provided. At weekends there was no prospect of stabling all its engines within the depot and still keep it fluid, and something like 20 were outstabled on a goods loop towards Craigentinny, complete with a round-the-clock steamraiser to look after the boilers.

Grantham with Class O2 2-8-0 No 63962 and an unknown WD 2-8-0 on the ashpits. It was not the most salubrious environment especially without mechanical handling equipment. The lifting gantry for dealing with hot axleboxes can just be seen behind the WD's tender.

Doncaster at the south end of the shed. Class 9F 2-10-0 No 92168 is on its home ground on the preparation pits. As usual the 2-10-0's ashpan side access doors are lying open!

Every shed had its idiosyncracies. In some cases they went far beyond that, to the point where working conditions were deplorable. This whole facet of railway operation was never accorded the attention and resources that its scale warranted. It is a sobering thought that in the 1950s there were LM Region depots with allocations of 50 engines and more which were devoid of any tools such as an electric drill or grinder! Yet vast sums of money were being spent on new locomotives, a considerable proportion of which were promptly employed on humble duties which any obsolete pre-grouping engine could have performed equally well. How much better it might have been to divert some of that money into modernising the depots at which the engines lived, notably to coaling and ash-handling plant, and perhaps to machine tools for routine maintenance. How many steam cleaning plants could have been installed for the cost of one Class 5? One is left with the inescapable conclusion that motive power depots were the Cinderellas of the railway. Could the use of that simple word 'shed' have been at the root of it?

173

An old fashioned hand coaling stage with
Class O2 2-8-0 No 63935 and an
unidentified WD 2-8-0 alongside. The
coal stage appears to have a built in water
column. Unfortunately this scene is
impossible to locate. The O2 has a tablet
catcher on the tender so was at some time
a Grantham engine.

Leeds Copley Hill, formerly Great
Northern Railway. Class A1 4-6-2 No
60133 Pommern is being coaled from an
old type stage using skips. Note the
accumulation of ash and clinker around
the ashpit. Stand pipes for hosing down
hot ashes are behind the crude screens.

York North shed, the roundhouse which was damaged by bombing in April 1942, with Britannia Class 4-6-2 No 70008 *Black Prince* from March and an indigenous WD 2-8-0 No 90217. The shed is nice and tidy although there is some water lying and the lighting has been recently renewed. This scene is now completely transformed for the building is part of the National Railway Museum, the Swannington winding engine occupying the corner behind No 90217.

York North with Class K1 2-6-0 No 62005 (50A York) on the turntable. The locomotive is now preserved on the North Yorkshire Moors Railway masquerading under various guises. As well as 62005, it has been seen as LNER 2005 and 62052. This site is also a part of the National Railway Museum.

York repair shop (rebuilt about 1957) which later became the diesel depot, finally closing in 1983. Class V2 2-6-2 No 60833 is standing with driving wheels out, possibly for attention to a hot axle box. No 60833 may have been involved in a derailment as the right hand lifeguard is bent back.

York North with Class 47 No D1991 then brand new, in April 1966. The coaling plant to the right was probably still in use, but only just. When removed a year or two later it proved very difficult to demolish even with explosives.

Gateshead from the west, showing the typical murky atmosphere of a steam shed. A magnificent NER bracket signal is to the right of the photograph. In the centre, beyond the office building is the manual coal stage, with the ashpits to the right. An unknown A1 Class Pacific (still with electric lighting) stands on the left.

Edinburgh Haymarket formerly North British Railway, the main shed for express passenger locomotives in the area serving Waverley. Class A4 4-6-2 No 60009 Union of South Africa is on the turntable but not yet coaled. That remaining on the tender looks pretty poor stuff. No 60009 is preserved in Scotland and has been running recently over BR tracks.

Edinburgh Haymarket about 1956. Class A2 4-6-2 No 60537 Bachelor's Button waits to use the turntable after LMS Class 5 4-6-0 No 45361.

Edinburgh Haymarket. A Class A4 4-6-2 with corridor tender takes water in the early 1960s; it is nicely cleaned as most of Haymarket's Pacifics usually were. The tender carries an electrification warning flash although it was unlikely that an A4 would trespass under the wires on the London Midland Region.

Haymarket in 1961. Class A3 4-6-2 No 60100 Spearmint *photographed immediately after fitting with trough type smoke deflectors. This was Driver Norman McKillop's regular engine. Later he wrote widely in railway periodicals under the pen-name 'Toram Beg'. A pair of Class 26s in the background were already stealing its main duties.*

Leeds Holbeck (20A later 55A) formerly Midland Railway. Jubilee Class 4-6-0 No 45597 Barbados *is tucked away in a corner of its home shed. The buildings are standard Midland 'square' roundhouses with cast iron window frames. The line in the background on viaduct is the LNWR 'new' approach to Leeds from Farnley Junction to the City station now used by Doncaster bound trains via the 1967 curve at Geldard Road. There is a fine collection of brake blocks and fire bars on the left.*

Leeds Holbeck with Jubilee Class 4-6-0 No 45697 Achilles under repair. This photograph was taken in the last days of steam and shows the locomotive minus nameplate and with a yellow band on the cab side indicating that it was prohibited under the 25kv overhead wires south of Crewe due to restricted clearances. This area of the shed is not remarkable for its tidiness. The pair of coupled wheels in the foreground are probably from an LMS Class 8F 2-8-0.

The end of steam. A very grimy trio at Leeds Holbeck in 1967. The Jubilee 4-6-0 No 45593 Kolhapur on the left has lost its name. The Class 5 4-6-0 is one of the earlier locomotives with domeless boiler.

Leeds, Holbeck. LMS Class 5 4-6-0 No 44662 resting at home between duties. There is a pile of LMS type arch bricks on the left and a fire cresset for men's warmth on the right. Sheds could be bitterly cold places in winter.

Leeds, Holbeck. A Class 9F 2-10-0 No 92122 taking (too much!) water. Note the frost fire adjacent to the water column. The structure on the right is the fuelling plant for diesel locomotives. The photograph dates from the early to mid 1960s when diesel and steam were running together.

Leeds, Holbeck. Inside one of the round-houses with a Fowler 2-6-4T, LMS Class 8F 2-8-0s and BR Crosti-boilered 2-10-0.

An unknown location but probably an ex LMS shed (and likely to be Leeds, Holbeck) from the design of the coaling plant. The number of the Class 9F 2-10-0 ends in 66 and it may therefore be one of the three fitted with mechanical stokers which worked between Birmingham and Carlisle.

Facing page, top:
Wakefield ex Lancashire & Yorkshire Railway shed, showing the improvements introduced by the LMS, the mechanical coaling plant left, ash disposal plant and vacuum operated turntable. A WD Class 8F 2-8-0 is leaving the turntable.

Facing page, bottom:
Wakefield with Jubilee Class 4-6-0 No 45596 Bahamas fitted with a double chimney, backing off turntable. Bahamas is now preserved at Dinting Railway Centre.

182

Edinburgh, St Margaret's, former North British Railway; a view of its main shed, still housing ex LNER Classes in some abundance. Note the GNR designed Class K2 2-6-0s. Class K2 2-6-0 No 61789 is passing on the down East Coast main line. This was a very congested site for the large number of locomotives allocated, 221 in 1954 less 43 at sub sheds. There was another shed on the up side, which housed shunting tanks, the original NBR shed and works. There was much local complaint here about smoke nuisance. The site is now covered by a modern office block.

Fort William, West Highland Railway, with a typical selection of West Highland motive power outside. From left to right they are a Class K2 2-6-0 (thought to be No 61782 Loch Eil), a Great Northern design imported by the LNER, a Class K4 three cylinder 2-6-0 built specially for the line by Sir Nigel Gresley, and an indigenous NBR 0-6-0, LNER Class J36, too dirty to read its number. There are two types of water columns visible, one with a swinging arm to the left and on the right an unusual design with two bays serving the tracks on each side.

184

*The rebuilt K4 now K1/1 2-6-0 No 61997
MacCailin Mor about to move off Fort
William shed sometime in 1952. Note the
high capacity aluminium wagons in the
background.*

185

Dumfries shed (ex G&SWR) with an assortment of BR standard, LMS and Caledonian engines taken probably in the mid 1950s. On the left is newly built 2-6-0 No 76072, then what appear to be Nos 44996, 57672, 57620, and with a stove-pipe chimney a CR Drummond standard goods.

Hawick ex North British Railway, the bank engine shed for assisting trains to Whitrope summit. In 1954, Hawick had a 100 per cent allocation of NBR locomotives. The J35 0-6-0 No 64494 and D30 4-4-0 No 62440 Wandering Willie carry targets, Nos 243 and 244, which suggests they were on banking duty. The Class D49 4-4-0 in the background, No 62719 Peebleshire was a visitor from Haymarket, no doubt off a terminating local from Edinburgh.

LOCOMOTIVE DEPOT ALLOCATION

The following tables show the allocation at depots involved with providing important contributions of power on the four groups of routes. They all apply to 1954, roughly a median point in Treacy's association with railways; the actual dates vary between January (LM Region) and October (NE Region) as available. At this time British Railways regional boundaries were still not clear-cut in the operating field, with 'penetrating lines' representing the old companies' incursions into territory which was the majority interest of others. This position was not regularised until February 1958, when, for instance, Kingmoor became an LM Region depot while Holbeck gravitated to the NE Region. This involved changes in motive power district boundaries and in shed codes.

The list of depots is by no means all-inclusive, and indeed is a little capricious. The intention has been to cover those depots whose engines were likely to regale Treacy in significant numbers at his various lineside photographic locations, and which prompted him to direct his camera at them. There are, therefore, some very significant omissions; Holyhead and Longsight do not appear, despite their haulage of the Irish Mail, the Comet and other expresses, though Blackpool, Newton Heath and Patricroft, all of which worked West Coast main line expresses, are included. By the same token, sheds like Watford and Bletchley, deeply involved with the Euston suburban services, find no place – Treacy seems to have ignored these stopping trains – while Oxenholme and Tebay, the small banking engine depots for Grayrigg and Shap banks, do. Some geographical regrouping of depots, notably in the Leeds area, has been indulged in across regional and district boundaries. The routes in Scotland used by the through Midland route trains, the G&SW line to Glasgow St Enoch and the Waverley route to Edinburgh, have been covered in the Midland table.

It will be seen that by 1954 the West Coast route had become an almost total preserve of post-1923 locomotive designs (recognising that four of these were direct Midland derivatives). The only significant exception was the ex-LNWR G2 0-8-0s, which were still hard at work on main line freight in similar numbers to those of the Stanier Class 8F 2-8-0s. The minor jobs kept a few ex-MR types going from Crewe southwards, while Lancashire depots held modest numbers of ex-L&YR 0-6-0s, both tender and tank. New locomotives with labour-saving fittings were engaged in a considerable proportion of very mundane work such as carriage shunting and short freight trips to shunt private sidings. The ex-LNWR small engines numbered no more than four, including a couple of 'Cauliflowers' at Penrith surviving on the CK&P line. In Scotland the tough little Caley 0-6-0s were still around in large numbers, often disfigured by stovepipe chimneys. The BR Standard engines comprised no more than a sprinkling. On the Midland the emphasis was more on the use of ex-MR 0-6-0s on the inferior work.

The LNER's building policies at Gresley's instigation resulted in a similar situation to that on the Midland, with little fluidity in allocation of the smaller pre-grouping engines. Large numbers of ex-GNR 0-6-0 tender and tank engines handled the local traffics and shunting as far north as Leeds; from there to the Scottish border this activity was the preserve of large numbers of ex-NER engines, with an important proportion – B16s and Q6s – still engaged on heavy main-line duty. A big depot like York had half its allocation in the form of ex-NER designs, and it was not unique. North British engines held sway as the secondary engines around Edinburgh. The GCR was represented only by pockets of O4 2-8-0s in the Doncaster area, A5 4-6-2Ts at Darlington and D11 Directors (built post grouping for Scotland) at Haymarket and Eastfield. There was some infiltration of modern ex-LMS designs here and there to meet special local conditions.

West Coast Routes   Allocation of Locomotives: early 1954

Shed Code	Total Allocation	Passenger Tender								Mixed Traffic Tender					MT Tank			Freight Tender			FT Tank	Other Steam					0-6-0 Shunter Diesel
		8P Duchess 4-6-2	8P Princess 4-6-2	7P Royal Scot 4-6-0	7P Reb. Jubilee & Patriot 4-6-0	6P Jubilee 4-6-0	6P Patriot 4-6-0	4P Compound 4-4-0	2P 4-4-0	6MT Clan 4-6-2	5MT 4-6-0	5MT 2-6-0	4MT 2-6-0	2MT 2-6-0	4MT 2-6-4T	3MT 2-6-2T	2MT 2-6-2T	8F 2-8-0†	7F 0-8-0 LNW G2	4F 0-6-0	3F 0-6-0T	Ex LMS	Ex LNWR	Ex MR	Ex L&YR	Ex CR	0-6-0 Shunter Diesel
1A Willesden	143					2	3				16	8		2	2	23		37	10	10	13						17
B Camden	55	15		12	7	8															13						
2A Rugby	88							7			38				9		1	10	11	2	4		1	5			
B Nuneaton	69								3			9	5			6	2	15	18		4			4	3		
3A Bescot	68										5	3	3					27	22		3			3			2
B Bushbury	38					9					4					5	1		7	3	4			3			2
D Aston	54										15	11		2	6	1			3	7				4			5
E Monument Lane	29								3		3				7	1				7			1	7			
5A Crewe North	107	9	8	17	3	8	12	5	9		31				3		2										
B Crewe South	119										24	23						19	3	4	18	1			6	3	18
8A Edge Hill	115		5	8	5	8	5				30				8			4	22		15				5		
B Warrington	55										10				2	2	3	8	5		10			10	5		
C Speke Junction	54											3						14	11		7				4		15
24E Blackpool	44					6					21			2	8		2								5		
26A Newton Heath	153					10					26	19		5	26	4		31	6§	2	2				22		
10A Springs Branch	64										11			3	11				23						8	8*	
B Preston	30				2	1			4		2			2					10		7	1			1		
C Patricroft	75					6			4		35					7			14		5				4		
11A Carnforth	43										18			6	3				6	4	6						
C Oxenholme	9														8						1						
D Tebay	10														4	1				5							
12A Upperby	91	5		3	2	8	8		5		38									5	13						4
C Penrith	6													3							1		2				
68A Kingmoor	150			16				2	3	5	55	27						10	13						7	10	2
D Beattock	12														7											5	
64D Carstairs	39								4		6				9			2								18	
66A Polmadie	178	9		5	5				2	5	12				45			5		2	5					83	
B Motherwell	104										15			5	7	1		15		1						60‡	

*Ex GCR J10

†Incl. WD 2-8-0 and 2-10-0

‡Incl. 1 Ex NBR J88

§Fowler Class 7F 0-8-0

East Coast Routes   Allocation of Locomotives: early 1954

Shed Code	Total Allocation	Passenger Tender					Mixed Traffic Tender									Mixed Traffic Tank				Freight Tender				FT Tank		Other Steam						0-6-0 Shunter, Diesel	ESI Bo-Bo, Electric
		A1 4-6-2	A3 4-6-2	A4 4-6-2	W1 4-6-2-2	D49 4-4-0	A2 4-6-2	V2 2-6-2	K1 2-6-0	K3 2-6-0	B1 4-6-0	5MT 4-6-0 LM	5MT 2-6-0 LM	4MT 2-6-0 LM	2MT 2-6-0 LM	L1 2-6-4T	V1/V3 2-6-2T	N2 0-6-2T	4MT 2-6-4T LM	O2 2-8-0	O4 2-8-0 GC	WD 2-8-0	J38/J39 0-6-0	J50 0-6-0T	J94 0-6-0ST	Ex LMS/LNE	Ex GNR	Ex GER	Ex GCR	Ex NER	Ex NBR		
34A Kings Cross	133		3	19				11			7					9		57									20					7	
B Hornsey	69																	14										52					3	
35A New England	168						9	23			17									19		42						52	1				5	
B Grantham	50	9	8				1													14							8	8	2				
36A Doncaster	173	8		1				21			23									35	4	14	8	1			52		6				
E Retford	70										6									17	9		8				23		7				
37A Ardsley	97	2						3			10										11		25	19		21		4	2				
B Copley Hill	40	10	4					3			7												1	7		8							
50B Neville Hill	71		5			4					13												11							38*			
50A York	159	5				7	8	30			15											10			9						75			
C Selby	54														7						1	3		3							2	38		
D Starbeck	32					16																		12								4		
51A Darlington	98		2						13		15			4	4ø	2	3		3						10	1				10	31		
H Kirkby Stephen	19															11																8		
52A Gateshead	94	14	9	8			4	12			8						7			7						2				23			
B Heaton	95	3	10				3	17	9					5			12					7			2					25			2
D Tweedmouth	31							6	8	4													7								6			
64A St Margarets	221					5		17	23	18	2	1			2		14				5	13				1			2	1	117		
B Haymarket	80	5	15	7		6	10	4			8						3													10	12		

*Incl. 5 Ex H&BR N13   øIncl. 1 BR Std. 3MT 2-6-0

Midland Route   Allocation of Locomotives: early 1954

Shed Code	Total Allocation	Passenger Tender							Mixed Traffic Tender						MT Tank			Freight Tender				FT Tank	Other Steam					Fell Main Line 2-D-2	0-6-0 Shunter Diesel
		7P Royal Scot 4-6-0	6P Jubilee 4-6-0	6P Patriot 4-6-0	4P Compound 4-4-0	2P 4-4-0	A3 4-6-2	D49 4-4-0	5MT 4-6-0	5MT 2-6-0	4MT 2-6-0	2MT 2-6-0	K3 2-6-0	B1 4-6-0	4MT 2-6-4T	3MT 2-6-2T	2MT 2-6-2T	Garratt 2-6-0 + 0-6-2	8F 2-8-0†	4F 0-6-0	J39 0-6-0	3F 0-6-0T	Ex LMS/LNE	Ex MR	Ex L&YR	Ex CR	Ex NBR		
14A Cricklewood	81										7	5				2	2		9	13		24	8						11
B Kentish Town	99		13		5				14						12	23				9		17	6						
15A Wellingborough	78																2	7	48	8		9	4						
B Kettering	42										8								22	5			7						
C Leicester	74				8	4			11		2				5	2	1		7	8		6	20						
16A Nottingham	140		6		7	11			7	2	3	1			11				24	33		5	21						9
17A Derby	139		4	1	6	6			19	3	4	2			6		1		11	28		4	41	2				1	
18A Toton	151																	18	66	28		3	26						10
22A Bristol	55		12		2				3						4	1				19		5	7	2					
21A Saltley	191				3	1			23	12	6				7	2			14	60		3	46						14
19A Sheffield	75								10	1	4	2							8	15		9	26						
B Millhouses	38		10		9	1			11	1							3						3						
20A Holbeck	93	8	18		6	2			25	3	3	3			3	1			12	5		4							
B Stourton	50											2							12	15		8		12					1
C Royston	61				1											4	3		24	9		6		14					
E Manningham	33				2	2			1			1			4	8	2			3		3		3	4				
F Skipton	39				2						2	3					3			15		4		10					
G Hellifield	18				1				2						4	2			2	5				2					
25G Farnley Junction	49		5		1				8	4							4		22			5							
68B Dumfries	38				4	3			3	6					2					1						19*		
A Corkerhill	92		6	9	15				11	4					14					5		1				27		
B Hurlford	61			1	24				2	5										6						20		3
68E Carlisle (Canal)	47						4	1	1				8	6							13						14		
64G Hawick	22																						1				21		

*Incl. 1 Ex-GER J69

†Incl. WD 2-8-0

Shed Code	Total Allocation	Pass Tender		Mixed Traffic Tender						MT Tank		Ft Tender	Freight Tank		Other Steam			
		6P Jubilee 4-6-0	4P Compound 4-4-0	K4 2-6-0	K1 2-6-0	B1 4-6-0	K2 2-6-0 GN	5MT 4-6-0 LM	4MT 2-6-0 LM	V1/V3 2-6-2T	4MT 2-6-4T LM	4F 0-6-0 LM	J50 0-6-0T	3F 0-6-0T LM	Ex NBR	Ex CR	Ex NER	Ex GCR
63A Perth	114	2	4					70		2		8			2	26		
60A Inverness	55							31						1		23		
B Aviemore	8							1								7		
65A Eastfield	139			4	3	17	12†	3	6	5				7	64		2	16
63D Fort William	12			2	2		5								3			

† includes 2 V4 2-6-2

Gateshead shed. The left hand locomotive is Class A3 4-6-2 No 60084 Trigo. The coal stage incline can be seen to the left of the ashpits, the rails showing copious use of sand by engines propelling locomotive coal to the top.